DUE TO
PUBLIC
WE AR
TO PU
NEW EDITION OF
LIFE BEFORE BIRTH
UNDER THIS
NEW TITLE OF:

THE CHILDREN THAT TIME FORGOT

Other books by Peter and Mary Harrison:

STAMP COLLECTING (Published by Barrie & Jenkins)
COINS AND BANKNOTES (Published by Barrie & Jenkins)
MAKE MONEY FROM YOUR CAR (Published by Kaye & Ward)
MYSTIC FORCES (Published by Sinclair Publishing)

Acknowledgements

The authors appreciate all the help received from people in the media who willingly gave of their time and energy to assist with the research of this book including newspaper reporters, radio and television producers, magazine editors, and secretaries of various organizations, also the Southend Police, the Bradford Archives, and countless members of the public.

A special mention must be given to the many people in the medical profession for their patience and advice, in particular Dr Peter Fenwick, Neuropsychiatrist, Inst. of Psychiatry, London, Dr Paul Pandarakalam of the Kottayam Medical College, South India, and Dr David Stevenson, Senior Lecturer in International Community Health at the Liverpool School of Tropical Medicine.

The religious chapter could not have been written without the co-operation of the various priests, vicars and spokesmen from all denominations especially Rabbi Louis Jacobs of St. Johns Wood, London.

A very special thanks must go to Miss Lorna Hinwood for her ingenious contribution.

Most of all we owe a tremendous vote of thanks to all the children and their relatives who were the essence of kindness and co-operation in the researching of the case histories.

Cover illustration by Margaret Massie-Taylor

We are presently researching our next book. If you have seen a ghost, please send your account of the sighting to us at the following address:

> PETER & MARY HARRISON
> 50 OXFORD STREET
> WELLINGBOROUGH
> NORTHANTS
> NN8 4JH

Peter and Mary Harrison

The Children That Time Forgot

Sinclair Publishing Ltd

A Sinclair Book

Copyright © Peter and Mary Harrison 1983

First published in Great Britain in 1983
(under the title of LIFE BEFORE BIRTH)
by Futura Publications, a Division of
Macdonald & Co (Publishers) Ltd
London & Sydney

This new edition published by
Sinclair Publishing Ltd 1989

British Library Cataloguing in Publication Data

Harrison, Peter
  The children that time forgot
  1. Reincarnation
  I. Title.   II. Harrison, Mary
  291.2'37

  ISBN 1-872149-01-4

Filmset, printed and bound in Great Britain by
BPCC Hazell Books Ltd Member of BPCC Ltd
Aylesbury, Bucks, England

To our late parents
Esme, Wilfred, Margaret and James

Sinclair Publishing Ltd
50 Oxford Street
Wellingborough
Northants
NN8 4JH

Contents

Introduction

Many people are so terrified at the prospect of death that they become introverted, despondent and victims of nervous tension, becoming totally incapable of relaxing and enjoying this life to the full.

The following case histories reveal a clue to the true nature of human consciousness, an indication that the personality exists not only on the Earth plane during our present lives, but also on a pre-birth dimension of time and space. Many children remember the days and months spent in their mother's womb before being born, and more amazingly, some remember further back than that to an existence before physical conception in a realm which, although similar to Earth in as much as this region contained houses, schools, rivers, trees, etc., differed in material density, i.e. life operated according to a different set of laws and principles to those vibrations by which life is lived on Earth.

The great majority of case histories deal with children's memories of former lives on Earth brought to the notice of their parents by spontaneous flashes, usually triggered off by some ordinary every-day activity or experience. In no case was hypnosis or any other form of age regression used, and in every case the parents were hesitant to jump to conclusions about their children's statements. Only after repeated spontaneous recollections of places, people and objects which were outside the knowledge of the children, did these parents concede that there might be an element of truth in their children's remarks.

It could be significant that in every case history, the child was pre-school age, almost all being two to three years of age when their memories were first voiced. By the time they reached six the memories seemed to vanish

Possibly by the time a child has learnt to speak coherently, these memories have already started to diminish, and by the time they reach school age their brains are so occupied with the increased amount of data to be absorbed that the pre-birth memories are pushed to the back of the brain into the subconsciousness.

According to the case histories there seems little doubt that in some instances life does indeed exist before Earthly birth, either in a non-physical realm, or on the physical material Earth plane. If this is so, then the idea of life after death seems like a natural following on and continuation of the personality.

If we have managed to spread the joyous message that physical death is not the end, then we have succeeded in our objective.

Part One

Case Histories

Life Before Birth
     and
Life After Death

Small girl remembers being killed by a train

Nicola Wheater, *Keighley*

Kathleen, mother of five-year-old Nicola, is convinced her child has lived before. From the age of two the child has been describing her previous life near the West Yorkshire village of Haworth, famous as the birth-place of the Brontë sisters, Charlotte, Emily and Anne, and where Emily's book *Wuthering Heights* is set.

The strange story began when Nicola was given a pull-along toy dog on her second birthday. The child got very excited as she told her mother, 'I'll call it Muff, the same as the other dog I had before.' Kathleen laughed at what she thought was the over-active imagination of her little girl. They had once owned a dog before, but never one called Muff. She played along with the child's game of make-believe, and agreed that Muff would make a lovely name for her little toy dog.

As the days went on, Kathleen noticed that Nicola became more and more engrossed with Muff and continually asked her toy dog if he could remember various incidents and experiences that they were supposed to have shared in the past. Assuming that it was all just a childish fantasy, Kathleen attached no importance to her daughter's so-called reminiscences, until suddenly Nicola asked her mother a strange question which made Kathleen stop and think. Being unusually articulate for her age, Nicola asked her mother, 'Why am I a little girl this time, Mummy? Why am I not a boy like I was before?'

When Kathleen asked Nicola what she meant, she answered, 'When Mrs Benson was my mummy I was a little boy and I played with Muff.' This remark left Kathleen puzzled, especially the reference to a Mrs Benson. Nicola did not know anyone called Mrs Benson, and in fact the name was not that of anyone known to the family.

As the references to what Nicola had done 'before' became more and more frequent, Kathleen was forced to take note of what her daughter was saying, as the child never varied her story, even slightly. Nicola insisted that she used to be a boy, and although she could not remember her Christian name, she knew that her second name had been Benson and that her mother had been known as Mrs Benson and her mother's first name had been something like Elspeth or Elsie. She was certain that she had lived near Haworth and that she had had two sisters and of course her pet dog Muff. She remembers that her father, Mr Benson, worked on the railway and that they lived in a little house near the railway lines.

She described the house in detail to her mother. 'It was grey stone in the middle of four houses joined together in a row. There were lots of fields at the back where I used to play with Muff.' Nicola was able to relate in the most amazing detail how her mother wore a long skirt: 'It was like a kind of pinny, just like the one that my doll wears.' She recalls how her mother wore her hair, and describes it as 'All tied up funny'. Her father wore big heavy boots and for some reason which Nicola has refused to talk about, she did not like her father much. 'He always had a dirty black face,' she tells, but when asked any other questions about Mr Benson she clams up.

She remembers sitting on the floor eating butties which her mother used to make for her and her friend who, along with Muff, was her constant companion. She knows her friend was another boy, but she cannot remember his name. 'He was smaller than me,' recalls Nicola, 'about one or two years smaller. Not one year and not two years,' she explains in an effort to describe her friend, 'and we always went to the railway together and we played in the fields behind my house.'

The little girl has vivid recollections of how as a boy she used to wander along the lanes and pathways surrounding her home with her beloved Muff. 'We played funny games all the time. I would throw my ball in the air and Muff would run and catch it and bring it back to me.'

Apparently her two sisters were much younger than Nicola, and she didn't have over-much to do with them, as would be the case with any other normal healthy little boy. 'They were too little for me,' she says, then adds 'One was just a baby and was too small to come out and play with me.'

Nicola told Kathleen of how her other Mummy always told her that she mustn't play on the railway; then she said, 'But I didn't listen to her and I used to go down to the railway with Muff and my friend.'

The child has clear memories of the day she was knocked down by a train. 'I was playing on the railway lines with Muff and my friend and I saw a man walking along swinging a lamp. After that a train came up fast and knocked me over.' When Kathleen asked her daughter what happened after that, Nicola replied, 'I got taken to hospital. Everyone kept asking me if I was all right but I couldn't walk or talk so I couldn't answer them.'

'What happened after that?' asked Kathleen.

'I went to sleep and died and I saw God in Heaven before I was born.' Then Nicola added, 'But I didn't really die. I came to you instead and you got to be my other Mummy.' When asked what God was like Nicola replied, 'I don't know how to say it to you. He was really beautiful but I don't remember what clothes he had on.' Then in an enthusiastic tone she assured her mother, 'He's much nicer than in his pictures.'

Because Nicola's story was so consistent, her mother decided to take her daughter to Haworth where they had never been before, in an attempt either to verify the little girl's words, or to put an end to the incredible story once and for all.

They travelled along desolate country lanes, through the bleak windswept moorland and Kathleen, who was unfamiliar with that part of the country, took a wrong turning and got hopelessly lost. Nicola, who like her mother had never been to the area before, came to the rescue, and directed Kathleen down some lonely unmarked roads straight into Haworth village. Nicola explained to her mother, 'I know the way because Muff and I used to walk all around here.'

After following Nicola's instructions, Kathleen was guided towards the outskirts of the village and was flabbergasted to find herself looking at what Nicola said was her other home: one of four old grey-stone terraced houses, exactly as Nicola had previously described and in the precise spot where the child said it would be. The physical details of the surrounding countryside matched Nicola's description perfectly, with the back of the house looking out over open fields. Kathleen noted that the address was 12 Chapel Lane, Oakworth.

Kathleen then went to the Haworth Parish Church to see if she could find any trace of a Benson family in the church records. The rector told her that she would be unlikely to find any Bensons in the parish registers as it was a very unusual name for those parts. However, he gave Kathleen permission to look through the birth and marriage registers, although he expressed his personal opinion that he thought the exercise would be a waste of time.

Kathleen's heart skipped a beat when she turned over the aging yellowed pages of an old birth register. Her eye caught the name Benson. The entry recorded the birth of a baby boy, John Henry Benson, on the 20th June, 1875. His father's name was given as Thomas Benson, whose occupation was a railway plate-layer. The boy's mother's name was given as Lucey Benson.

Kathleen looked down at little Nicola's face, then at the register of births, wondering if her daughter and the baby John Henry could really be one and the same person. The mother's name, Lucey, caused Kathleen to wonder even more. Nicola was of the opinion that her previous mother had been called Elspeth or Elsie. Could there be some mistake due to the similarity of the words Elsie and Lucey? The father's occupation as a railway plate-layer tied in with Nicola's story, a plate-layer being someone who lays the tracks down on the railway.

A further line of research provided even more startling results. In the Archives Department at the City of Bradford Metropolitan Council offices, the reference librarian, Mr Ian Dewhirst, has in his charge the census for the Haworth district. By law, the census, which is taken only once in every ten years, must remain confidential for a hundred years, so the latest details which could be consulted were the results of the 1881 census. The following information came to light:

12 Chapel Lane, Oakworth

		Age		Born
Thomas Benson	Head	29 yrs	Railway Plate-layer	Kildwick (Yorks)
Susy(?) Benson	Wife	30 yrs		Bradford (Yorks)
Hephyibah(?) Benson	Daughter	3 yrs	Scholar	Keighley (Yorks)
Sellis Benson	Daughter	6 mths		Keighley (Yorks)

The most significant point about the above entry is that although it represents the same Benson family of 12 Chapel Lane, Oakworth, as mentioned in the Haworth church birth register, there is no mention of the son John Henry. As it was required by law that each and every member of the family must be included in the census, this means that the boy John Henry must have died before the census was taken in 1881.

Taking into account the fact that Nicola remembers having had two sisters when she lived before as a boy and that the second Benson daughter Sellis was only six months old when the 1881 family details were recorded, this points to John Henry's death being between 1880 and

1881, when the child would have been between five and six years of age.

Unfortunately the hospital for the Haworth/Oakworth area in 1880–81 has long been closed down and so it is impossible to check to see if there had ever been any record of a child having been admitted after being knocked down by a train.

Again there is some discrepancy regarding the name of the mother. The census seems to show Thomas Benson's wife as Susy, but according to Ian Dewhirst, there is some doubt attached to this. The entries are in handwriting which is very difficult to decipher. He thinks the handwriting gives the name of Susy, but he does admit that it could just as easily be Lusy with a flourishing capital L. He goes on to remark that the Bensons seemed to go in for unusual names for their children, i.e. Hephyibah and Sellis, and he adds that he's not entirely sure that he read the name Hephyibah correctly. This highlights the problem of having to depend upon roughly written documents in order to establish the facts.

Let us for a moment suppose that the census entry for Thomas Benson's wife is Lucy. This would fit in with the entry in the Haworth birth register of Lucey: the same name with a different spelling. However, this still doesn't resolve the matter of Nicola thinking that her previous mother's name was Elsie. Perhaps buried in the store of information in young Nicola's unconsciousness is the name Lucy, but her conscious mind has interpreted the name as Elsie.

One thing which is very much to the fore of Nicola's consciousness is the terrifying experience of being knocked down by a train. Kathleen explains how one night the family were sitting together watching a film on television called *The October Man*, starring John Mills. There was a sequence in the film where a man was standing on top of an old railway bridge ready to throw himself down on to the railway lines. There was a shot of a train thundering down the railway track, and instantly

16

Nicola started to scream hysterically. She threw herself down on to the carpet gasping for breath and throwing her arms in the air wildly. Her mother thought that the child was having a fit or a heart attack and rushed to help her. Little Nicola could not be consoled, and cried out, 'The train, the train', repeatedly. It was only when her mother switched the television off that the child calmed down.

'She seemed to be re-living the time when the train knocked her down,' explains Kathleen. 'I had no idea that the film would have affected her like that.'

One possible explanation for Nicola's story, unless, of course, it is truly a straightforward example of reincarnation, is that it could be a case of temporary spirit over-shadowing, which is not to be confused with spirit possession, whereby the spirit of a member of the 19th century Benson family has latched on to young Nicola. But Nicola's strange behaviour when she watched the train on television thunder down the track would seem to point to a more personal involvement, and would suggest that she was re-living a terrible past experience, so overwhelming that it caused her to go into a convulsion-like frenzy.

Nicola's mother is in no doubt whatsoever that her daughter's story points to reincarnation. Kathleen did not know of the research being carried out at the Archives Department in Bradford, and when she was told that Nicola's story did in fact check out and that the boy John Henry who had lived in the old grey-stone house had been killed before the 1881 census had been taken, and that his father had worked on the railway she became absolutely convinced that Nicola had been re-born. 'I always thought that she was telling the truth. I realized that if she was making it up, the story would probably alter, but it never did. Now I know the results of the census I know she has been telling the truth. There is no explanation of how she could have had so many details in her head of a place she had never ever seen in her life.'

As far as Nicola herself, now a bubbly cuddly five-year-old with chubby rosy cheeks and a head of tousled golden curls, is concerned, the nicest thing she remembers about her previous life is all the fun she had with Muff.

Girl remembers her own funeral

Mandy Seabrook, *Hitchin*

Gillian had just finished her usual afternoon cup of coffee when she felt the stab of her first contraction. A gush of excitement rushed through her as she realized that at last the long months of waiting were over. Already her mind was buzzing with visions of how she would enjoy the late summer with her new baby. Like any happy mother-to-be she carefully checked over the little pastel-coloured baby clothes she had so lovingly set aside in preparation for the great day.

A short time later, after a perfectly normal labour, a beautiful baby girl was born in the modern delivery room of the Women and Children's Hospital in Leeds. The baby's parents were over-joyed as they welcomed the child into the world, and her four-year-old sister Carol was bubbling with excitement at the prospect of having a real live baby to play with. During that first euphoric day there was a stream of friends and relatives armed with flowers and baby cards, all showering their congratulations on the proud family.

Unfortunately the celebrations were short lived. When the baby was given the routine medical inspection by the hospital paediatric doctor, Gillian's smiles dissolved into tears as she was told that little baby Mandy had been born with a double hernia behind the heart. The infant was moved to the intensive care unit where she was given constant attention by the nursing staff. The following few days were like a nightmare for the parents, who hovered between hope and despair as they listened to the doctors whose responsibility it was to prepare such parents for any frightening developments which might occur. The distraught mother and father were forced to face the fact that they might lose their precious new-born baby.

However, the crisis eventually passed and much to the relief of her parents, little Mandy's condition became stable and she started to gain weight, the first sure sign of improvement. She was discharged from hospital and the family settled down to a normal existence.

Five months later the baby caught a common cold, and although her mother was somewhat alarmed by this, her fears soon subsided as she watched her tiny daughter bounce back to relative good health again, after only two days. Mandy appeared to be particularly exuberant during this period, so much so that the child's grandmother who was a nurse, made the prophetic remark 'I've seen babies like that before. They get energetic before they die.' The chilling words pierced Gillian's heart.

Later that afternoon, the child's mother thought that she had heard a choking sound. She rushed to the cot and was horrified to find that her baby's face had turned purple and she was gasping for breath. An alarm call went out for the family doctor who came immediately. He examined little Mandy and informed Gillian that her child had just suffered a severe heart attack. Even as he spoke, the life was ebbing from the tiny body.

Suddenly the heartbeat and pulse stopped completely. The doctor's grim expression told Gillian that the end had come. As she stared at her baby in stunned silence, Gillian saw the doctor bend over the child, force her tiny lips apart, and breathe deeply into her mouth. Tears of joy streamed down Gillian's face as she saw her infant's chest start to rise and fall in response to the doctor's kiss of life. She took the daughter who had come back from the dead into her arms and held the fragile frame close to her heart in an attempt to regulate the baby's heartbeat by using her own heart as a pace-maker. Mandy's face had become relaxed and her eyes were open, staring up at her mother.

Sadly, the reprieve lasted for only a few short minutes. 'I kissed her, but when I looked down at her eyes I realized that they had gone dry. I knew she had slipped away.' A second heart attack had taken the baby's life. The doctor tried mouth-to-mouth resuscitation again, but without success. The baby lay dead in her mother's arms and it seemed like the end of the world to Gillian.

Mandy's death had a chaotic effect on her family. The months of worry and anxiety had taken their toll on her parents' relationship which had been slowly deteriorating. While the baby's life had tottered precariously in the balance, the couple had managed to put their differences to one side, but when the slender bonding thread was severed, their relationship suffered irredeemable damage and they decided to go their separate ways.

Gillian, her heart heavy with bereavement and the break-up of her home, tried desperately to pick up the pieces of her shattered life. She became acquainted with a kindly sympathetic man called George Seabrook, on whom she started to rely more and more. Eventually she married George and once again her existence took on a semblance of harmony and normality. Like Gillian, George had also been through a traumatic time and had recently become divorced. Determined to put their troubles behind them, they made a pact that no mention would be made of the past. They agreed to make a fresh start.

The couple had four children: Wendy, Sean, John, and the fourth, another girl, born in May, 1972, they decided to call Mandy, after the baby who had died, because the new baby looked remarkably like the first Mandy, with bright blue eyes and jet-black pupils. They were adamant, however, that they should adhere to their agreement not to tell their children about the first Mandy.

One day, two years later, the Seabrooks were travelling from Leeds down the M1 motorway on a family outing. It was a sunny spring afternoon. Little Mandy was sitting on her mother's knee in the front passenger seat of the car and the other children were singing songs in the back seat. They passed the cemetery where the first Mandy had been buried, at Hunslet on the outskirts of the city, an area totally unknown to the children who had never been taken to that part of the city before.

Mandy suddenly jumped up from her mother's lap. 'Look, Mummy,' she cried excitedly, pointing through the car window. 'That's the place you put me in the ground that time, and you nearly fell on top of me, remember?' Her parents looked at each other in absolute horror, neither of them able to utter a word. 'Mandy sent shivers up my spine,' recalls Gillian, who had been so upset over the loss of the first Mandy that she had always found it impossible to talk about her. George who was at the driving wheel remembers that he got such a shock that the hairs at the back of his neck stood up on end. 'I felt as if I'd been struck by an electric current,' he recollects. 'There was just no way that my little girl could have known anything about the cemetery, its location, or any of the other details.'

Mandy then went on to describe a tiny silver bracelet engraved with crosses, roses and words which she remembered wearing in her coffin. This bracelet had been fastened round Mandy Number One's tiny wrist when she was buried. It was indeed silver, engraved with roses and crosses. It had been given to the first Mandy as a present from the brother of the first baby's father, a man called Patrick whom the second Mandy never knew. Mandy remembered that the bracelet had words on it. The inscription read: 'To darling Mandy from Uncle Patrick.'

At the time of the first Mandy's death, Gillian had been treated for shock by her doctor and had been given some tablets to help calm her down. She remembers being in a state near to collapse while standing at her baby's grave and with the combination of the tablets and grief, she lost her balance, slipped on the wet soil and in fact almost fell into the grave on top of the miniature white coffin.

Before the lid of the coffin was closed on the baby, it was noticed that a tiny half tooth had cut through the gum on the bottom left hand side. Another thing noticed was a solitary curl on the crown of the baby's head, but no sign of any other hair. When Mandy Number Two was born, the same half tooth was visible on the bottom left hand side of her gum and the same solitary curl crowned her head, although there was no sign of any other hair at birth.

In spite of Mandy Number Two's striking resemblance to the first Mandy, and the fact that the tooth and curl were present at birth, the family didn't think that there was anything strange about it at the time. As Gillian says, 'We weren't looking for a connection between the two Mandys. None of us believed in reincarnation and it wasn't until much later that we began to see that there might be a connection between the two girls.'

The second Mandy has since grown into a bright energetic girl with a happy-go-lucky disposition. She sports long shining brown hair, straight as a poker, but for the one solitary curl which can still be seen on the crown of her head.

When Mandy Number Two was three years old, she was walking with her father across the forecourt of Leeds railway station. They were making their way to the coffee bar when Mandy caught sight of a boy in a wheelchair being pushed through the bustling crowds. She suddenly turned to her father and said, 'Stevie's OK and he can walk now.'

George Seabrook was astounded at these words because unknown to Mandy he had had a spastic son by his previous marriage called Stephen who had died when Mandy was just a few months old. He had never even mentioned Stephen's name to his daughter or to any of the other children because of the agreement which he and Gillian had come to when they married, whereby they had decided to put their past lives behind them. The spastic child had never lived with him but had been cared for by his former wife's parents. The name of Stephen was more or less taboo.

When Mandy mentioned Stevie, George Seabrook was so incredulous that he got Mandy to explain her remark, asking her, 'What do you mean, love? What Stevie?'

She answered, 'You know, your own Stevie. Stephen. He can walk now.'

Bearing in mind that Mandy had never been told about Stephen's existence, Mr Seabrook was thunderstruck, most of all by the words 'He can walk now'. The child was too young to understand what spastic meant. He also wondered at Mandy referring to the boy as Stevie, the name by which George had always called his son.

Just before Mandy's fifth birthday, Gillian was preparing lunch in the kitchen when her small daughter ran in and tugged at her skirt.

'Mummy, why did you cry when I died?' she asked.

Gillian replied, 'But you're not dead, darling.'

Mandy persisted. 'Oh, you remember, Mummy, when I was very little. I couldn't live long because I was poorly. Now I've come back. I'm Mandy Number Two.'

There is a twist to this story. The first Mandy's sister Carol had only just reached her fifth birthday when the baby had died. Carol had not long started school, and on the day of the funeral it was thought best that the child should be sent to school as usual.

When Gillian later married George Seabrook, Carol was naturally included as part of the family. The crucial question arises: could Carol have related the story to Mandy about having had a baby sister called Mandy who died? That two half sisters, one a two-year-old toddler, and the other an eleven-year-old girl, could have had such conversations is physically possible, but is it logically probable?

In the first place, Carol was not at the funeral and was never told the location of the cemetery, so there is no explanation for Mandy's first statement about being put in the ground. Bear in mind that the child was in a fast car on a motorway, and they passed the cemetery in a flash, yet it was in that same lightning flash that the two-year-old pointed towards the graveyard and announced, 'That's the place you put me in the ground that time.'

Secondly the child Carol was not at the funeral service, so she did not witness her mother almost falling into the grave. It is hardly feasible that this kind of information would be passed on to a five-year-old child. There still remains the possiblity that Carol had overheard a conversation regarding the grave-side mishap, lodged this information in her brain, then fed it into the second Mandy's brain to be used at the appropriate time, either wittingly or unwittingly.

The main obstacle to this line of reasoning is the time factor involved. When Mandy Number One was buried, Carol had just reached her fifth birthday. When Mandy Number Two made her first statement in the car as they passed the graveyard, Carol was eleven and Mandy was two. Even if the toddler had been carefully tutored by her half-sister, would a child of this age act perfectly on cue and make her statement at precisely the moment when the car flashed passed the cemetery? Remember, Mandy was in the front of the car on her mother's lap, and the other children were in the back of the car taking part in a sing-song at the time. Would the child then follow up her first remark with the accurate statement about how her mother almost fell into the grave? This seems unlikely, and considering that Carol did not attend the funeral and did not know where the cemetery was, impossible.

Thirdly, there is the matter of the eyes, tooth, and the curl. There is no possible way that Carol could have had any influence whatsoever over Mandy Number Two's physical traits.

Again, how can this explanation be applied to the remarks about George Seabrook's son Stephen? Stephen was the child of Mr Seabrook and his first wife. Mandy was the child of Mr Seabrook and his second wife. Mandy had never met, or known about, Stephen, who died when she was only four months old. In addition, there are the words 'He can walk now'. How can these be explained?

And now to the tail piece. George Seabrook had been collecting cardboard milk bottle tops, and one day he gave them to the children to play with. Gillian, who was busy with the household chores at the time, remarked casually to the children that the cardboard milk bottle tops could

25

be used to make pom-poms or fluffy wool balls. Immediately Mandy asked her mother why she had buried her other fluffy wool ball. At first Gillian did not know what Mandy was talking about, and being engrossed in her washing up, she vaguely replied, 'It must be in the garden, love,' thinking to herself that if some toy or another had been buried, then the garden would seem the obvious place to look.

Mandy would not be fobbed off and insisted that her mother had buried her fluffy ball.

'What fluffy ball are you talking about, Mandy?' asked her mother.

'You know, the yellow one. The one that you put in the ground with me,' came Mandy's reply.

Gillian's mind raced back to the time of the first Mandy's funeral. Little Carol had just started school and had been taught how to make fluffy wool balls. She brought the little ball home from school as a present for her baby sister. The baby died, and Carol had asked her mother if she could still give the present to Mandy. She wanted to put the fluffy wool ball into the coffin but Gillian had decided against the idea and said 'No'. As far as everyone knew, that was the end of it.

When Mandy Number Two mentioned the fluffy ball being put in the ground with her, Gillian had only one course of action. She asked Mandy to go and find Carol who was not in the room at the time and had had no part in the foregoing conversation.

Carol was duly brought before her mother and was asked to try to remember when the first Mandy had died. She was then asked to describe what really happened to the fluffy wool ball. Carol admitted that although she had been told that the ball should not go into the coffin with the baby, she managed to hide the ball underneath the dead baby when no one was looking. The coffin lid had been left open for a whole day and night, so there would have been ample opportunity for the girl to accomplish this without being noticed by anyone, especially when

26

the household was in such disarray. Her mother was in a state of shock at the time, and would not have been watching Carol's every move. The yellow fluffy wool ball was in fact buried with baby Mandy, against Gillian's wishes.

Gillian says that Mandy has an unnerving habit of dropping reminders of the past, completely out of the blue. When she was six, she said to her mother, 'Do you remember the night I died? There was a bright star shining in the sky.' Her mother turned her mind back to the time she had tried so hard to forget. 'Suddenly it came back to me,' says Gillian. 'I had gone to close the curtains when I saw an unusually bright star hovering over the garden. I commented on it at the time because it was so bright and so low. But after that I never gave it another thought. Then Mandy said, "That was *my* star. It was my way of telling you that I would be back".'

Mandy is quite matter-of-fact about her previous life. She says, 'I remember very well when I was Mandy One, but I didn't like it when everyone cried when I died. It was nice to come back.'

Mandy's father, George Seabrook, a sensible, level-headed man, used to be extremely sceptical about such matters. 'I used to think when you're dead you're dead and that's the end of it, but I don't think that now. I know in my heart that my little girl has lived before.'

Says Gillian, 'We really are convinced that Mandy has been reborn. They say that after you've lost a child, having another baby fills the gap, but it doesn't. Admittedly it takes your mind off it a lot, but it never makes up for the loss. I withdrew into myself and would not talk to anyone for days on end. If I had known then that Mandy would come back, I might have been much more philosophical about her death, though if someone had told me that all this would happen, I wouldn't have believed it possible. I certainly believe it now.'

Boy remembers assassination of Thomas Becket

Philip Harding, *Milton Keynes*

As a special treat, two-and-a-half-year-old Philip was taken on a day outing to Oxford by his Aunt Rosemary. The child had never been to Oxford in his life, and Rosemary had only been there once before when she passed through the town on a coach trip.

They set off on a bright sunny morning and no sooner had they arrived in Oxford when little Philip asked his aunt, 'Can we go and see the clock, Aunty Rosie?'

Thinking it was just idle chatter Rosemary humoured the child by saying that they would probably pass a clock on the way. Philip answered, 'But I mean the funny clock.' His aunt asked him, 'What funny clock?' Philip then gave a full description to his aunt of a large clock on the side of an old church which had strange markings on the face.

'I always went to see the funny clock,' said Philip. Rosemary explained to him that he couldn't have seen any clock in Oxford because he had never been there before. The child told her, 'I saw it when I lived here when I was Andrew.'

'Of course I thought he was just talking a lot of rubbish,' said Rosemary, 'especially as the so-called clock he described to me was so off-beat. By what he said it sounded to me more like a sun dial.'

Rosemary then suggested that they should go shopping, but Philip became very upset and started to cry, saying that he really wanted to see his clock again. Rosemary remembers, 'He looked so dejected that I started to wonder what was going on. There was definitely something niggling him.'

In spite of Rosemary's promises of ice-cream and sweets

when they went shopping, Philip would not be moved. He only wanted to see his clock, which he said was on the old church. 'I felt helpless as I didn't know what to do or where to turn to,' she says. Then Rosemary told Philip, 'I don't know where your clock is, love.'

Philip sparked up and replied, 'I know where it is. I'll show you.'

Philip took his aunt's hand and led her all round the side alleys and back streets of Oxford. 'He seemed so intent on finding his clock and he was so definite in leading me round the streets that I just resigned myself to go along with it. All of a sudden there it was. The old church and the most peculiar looking clock I've ever seen in my life. I couldn't believe my eyes.'

Philip had taken his Aunt Rosemary to the old clock, which was exactly as he had described it to her. Rosemary explains, 'It was the strangest thing in the world, because I thought that Philip's description was bound to be completely out as I thought that he'd got it all mixed up, but he was absolutely correct. The clock had a large sundial incorporated onto the face, as well as the regular hands and numbers. That was why Philip's description sounded confused!'

When Rosemary asked Philip how he knew about the clock he assured her that he remembered it from when he lived before as a little boy called Andrew.

Rosemary never told anyone at all about what Philip had told her – not even his parents. 'I knew that it would sound so far-fetched that they would probably think I was going crazy.'

About a year later when Rosemary was looking after Philip for his parents he suddenly said, 'When I was Andrew I saw Thomas Becket being assassinated.'

Rosemary was astounded because although the Andrew part was not a surprise to her, she just couldn't believe that she had heard the words 'Thomas Becket' – and 'assassinated'. These words were totally outside the range of the three-year-old's vocabulary and the historical event was beyond the horizon of his knowledge. 'I could hardly speak I got such a shock,' says Rosemary. Philip told his aunt that when he was Andrew he was bigger than he is now because he was six years old and he could write.

Philip says, 'I wrote down everything I saw. I had lots of notebooks then but I think they got lost.' The child remembers that he had been taken to Canterbury for some reason from his home in Oxford, and it was during this visit to the city that the archbishop was murdered. He remembers seeing lots of people rushing about and he especially remembers that there were lots of soldiers in the city. He says, 'The soldiers had giant swords and big long shields with drawings on them and they wore funny masks on their faces. Some of them were on fancy horses and some were just standing about. They were very noisy and shouted a lot.'

Philip says that at the time of the murder he was actually in Canterbury Cathedral. 'Lots and lots of people were there,' he says. He remembers the clothes that the people wore: he describes them as 'long dresses'. He told his aunt, 'The men wore short dresses and the ladies wore long ones.'

It seems that although he had only been six years old at the time, the little boy was acutely aware that something terrible was taking place. He says, 'I knew it was a very bad thing and that's why I wrote it in my notebook. There was lots of noise and screams in church. It was very dark and I couldn't see very well. I was squashed with all the people. I couldn't see Thomas Becket because the big people were in front of me but I know that he was there and the soldiers murdered him then they ran out.' After that, Philip says, 'Everybody was pushing and screaming and frightened.'

When Philip described the scene to his Aunt Rosemary there was no doubt in her mind that her nephew's memories were real, and that he had lived before in the 12th century. 'No child of his age could have such knowledge of events which took place so long ago. We never discuss history or anything like that – we're just not that kind of family – and in any case we would never talk about a murder in front of a three-year-old child. As for Thomas Becket, I don't think any of us know anything about him. I just know that he existed once and that he was murdered but I've got no idea of how or why. In fact I know nothing at all about the man.'

Rosemary says, 'I think the whole thing is a bit creepy. The thing that puzzles me most is that when Philip first mentioned Becket he used the word assassination, not murder, which would be more like the thing a kid would say, and what's more, he seemed to know exactly what assassination meant.'

There is one link with Oxford in the story of Thomas Becket. Robert of Cricklade, prior of St Frideswide's in Oxford from 1140 to 1180, wrote the life of Thomas Becket but since the prior would not have been married it is unlikely that he would have been in the company of a six-year-old boy at the time of the murder. It is more probable that Andrew was one of the congregation gathered for the service on that fateful winter evening in 1170. The events of that night made such an impression on the young mind that they are still vivid more than 800 years later.

Girl remembers being a nineteenth-century nurse

Angela Mahony, *Poole*

Angela Mahony was born in Cork in the South of Ireland and when she was twenty-two months old her parents moved to Poole in Dorset, England. This was the first time Angela or her parents had been outside Ireland. In fact baby Angela had never even been outside her native city of Cork. It took a few days for the family to settle in to their new home, but on the third day Angela's mother Kathleen thought she would take her little girl on a walk round Poole to look at the shops.

On that very first visit they passed Barclay House, the huge bank building. The child became very excited and started to shout out wildly, 'Look, Mummy, that's my hospital. That's where I was a nurse.'

Her mother explained to the child that the big building was not a hospital but the office of a large bank. She told Angela that the people in the bank look after other people's money. Then she said to her daughter, 'So you see, Angie, they don't have any nurses in there.'

Angela would not accept her mother's explanation but got more and more excited and repeated her first statement, saying, 'It is a hospital.' Then pointing towards the building she added, 'I was a nurse in there when I was here before.'

Her mother asked her what she meant, reminding Angela that they had only been in the country three days and that this was the first time that either of them had ever walked down that particular road. Angela then said, 'When I was a nurse I always came down this road with my long dress on and my nurse's hat.' She described her uniform as being long, with a long white apron and a funny-shaped hat.

Kathleen took the child home and thought no more about what the child had said, but a few days later when they passed Barclay House for the second time, Angie again became highly excitable and repeated her story about having lived before as a nurse.

This time Angela's father Desmond was with them. When he heard his little girl's remarks he turned to his wife and asked, 'What's she on about?' Kathleen told him what had happened on their previous walk past the bank building.

'But that's ridiculous,' said Desmond. 'Where did she pick up stuff like that?'

Kathleen told her husband that she was just as puzzled as he was and that since they had no friends or relatives who were nurses Angela couldn't have been told anything about them. 'Besides,' said Kathleen, 'she seems to recognize this area and she insists that there should be a hospital here.'

Desmond is a man who likes to get to the bottom of things, so he asked Angela, 'What's all this silly stuff you've been telling Mammy, Angie? You know you've never been a nurse, darling. Have you been playing at nurses with your dollies?'

Angela was quite definite in her reply to her father. She told him, 'Not with my dollies, Daddy, with big people.' Then again she pointed towards the bank building and said, 'It was in there when I was here the last time. That's where I was a nurse.'

From that day on every single time the child passed the bank building she said the same thing. As the months went on and little Angela's speech became more coherent she was able to communicate more and more details of her past life to her bewildered parents. She said that she had a lot of sick people to look after and she had to work very long hours. Angela remembers that she did her share of night duty and she told her mother, 'Sometimes I had to sit up all night to look after the sick people. It was very dark and I didn't like it much.'

33

Because Angela never changed her story her mother wonders if there might be something in her little girl's memories. Kathleen says, 'It makes me wonder because Angie has never said anything else remotely like her story about having been a nurse. If she was always making up yarns about herself then of course I would just put it all down to fantasy. But she has always given the exact same account of her days as a nurse and has never come out with any similar stories about other lives. So I'm inclined to believe that she really does remember something from her past.'

Kathleen says that all mothers are well aware of how their children can lapse into little day-dreams and at times they can come out with the most far-fetched stories. 'The thing about this,' says Kathleen, referring to Angela's story, 'is that they always forget things and when they repeat the story they either leave some of their previous details out or else they get completely muddled up and invariably you end up with about four or five versions of the same story. That's always the give-away. But whenever Angie talks about being a nurse the story never alters. That's why I feel that her memories are real and she is not just making it up.'

On researching Angela's story, it was found that totally unknown to the child's parents, next to the site presently occupied by Barclay House there used to be an old workhouse. It was known as the Union Workhouse and it was built in 1838, and of course, as in all workhouses, nurses were employed in the building to take care of the sick. It was then discovered that in 1900 the workhouse was converted into an infirmary. The guardians of the infirmary are on record as having stated that they were 'very particular about the calibre of nurses they employed'.

The infirmary eventually became part of the old Poole hospital, which in those days was known as 'The Cornelia Hospital' after Lady Cornelia Wimborne who financed it.

So Angela could well have worked as a nurse in any one of the three establishments – the workhouse, the infirmary or the Cornelia hospital. There was a large turnover of nurses through the Poor Law system which governed the workhouse and the infirmary. The minimum age for a nurse employed in the workhouse was set at twenty-five in 1873. In 1900 when the workhouse was converted to an infirmary the age restriction for nurses was lowered to twenty-one, and nurses were not allowed to continue their employment when they married.

Although general conditions in Poor Law workhouses were very rough up and down the country, on the inmates and on the nursing staff alike, the Poole workhouse had a better reputation than most. The children were treated slightly better than in many workhouses and they received more individual attention. They were taught net-making and were kept occupied at producing nets for Poole's considerable fishing trade with Newfoundland and Labrador.

A young girl wishing to enter the nursing profession in those days could do so either by being accepted as a trainee in a teaching hospital, where she would take a three year course, or she could go directly to the workhouse as an untrained assistant.

Normally the workhouses would be run by a master and matron, usually a husband-and-wife team who took care of the all-over day-to-day running of the building, the master being responsible for the incoming stores and goods and the matron – who was really more of a housekeeper – supervising the laundry, food, hygiene, etc. However the nursing division was run on an independent system within the workhouse. A superintendent nurse was in charge of all the nursing administration and activities and she took the role of the present-day matron. She was usually a fully-trained nurse of good education and social standing in the true tradition of Florence Nightingale.

The superintendent nurse took charge of all the trainee and assistant, or half-trained nurses, and she generally was able to command respect from nursing staff, doctors and patients alike.

In the early days of the workhouse the nurses were more often than not the inmates themselves. Many kindly souls, known as pauper nurses, who were half dying themselves of a multitude of diseases, were left to care for their companions in conditions of squalour. These untrained, diseased women had to cope with every type of illness and they also acted as midwives. It was only when many new-born babies were discovered to be suffering from high temperatures and diseased eyes that measures were taken to improve the system.

It was difficult to effect any improvements within the Poor Law system to the workhouses, not least because these establishments were houses of deterrent for people convicted of various crimes. In many cases it was argued by the workhouse guardians that the conditions in the workhouses, however shabby and unhygienic, were far superior to the homes that some of the inmates had come from. The guardians were afraid that if the workhouses were improved to the degree whereby the inmates were more comfortably cared for and better fed than in their own homes, then the buildings would cease to be effective in as much as they would no longer deter would-be offenders. For this reason, life in the workhouse was kept to such a standard as to bring the inmates to task and to have a punishing effect on them.

The few trained nurses had been paid such low wages that they usually left the workhouse system to go on to the better conditions offered by the infirmaries and voluntary hospitals. Such nurses looked upon their stint in the workhouse just as a stepping stone towards a more lucrative career in private nursing. The standard wage for a union workhouse nurse and trainee at a teaching hospital in 1849 was an incredible five shillings per week (equivalent to 25 pence). Because the nurses were supplied with food and accommodation of sorts, the five shillings was not looked upon as a wage, but as mere pin money.

The idea was to attract young women of stable financial backgrounds to the nursing profession, and to discourage girls from becoming nurses for the wrong reasons. Although fine enough in theory, this did not quite work out as expected in practice because many young girls of sub-standard education looked upon the nursing profession as nothing more than a way of filling in their time before marriage. Because of the shortage of nurses the standards in the workhouses were so low that at one time the only requirement for a nurse was that the girl be educated enough to read the doctor's prescription.

Such women were a thorn in the flesh of the newly thriving nursing profession in England. They often treated their patients with downright cruelty and were inclined to look upon the inmates as prisoners who did not deserve any decent treatment. This attitude became so widespread amongst untrained nurses that a rule was passed to demand that workhouse patients should be treated in accordance with their disease, and not in accordance with their morals. After this the cruelty to patients by the untrained nurses was replaced by what was described as passive cruelty whereby certain patients were more or less ignored and left to suffer unattended.

There was a stigma attached to unmarried mothers and they would be given a particularly rough time in the workhouse. Their hair would be cut in a short cropped style and they were invariably made to wear a straight yellow sack-cloth which was the sign of a fallen woman. Even amid the unsavoury community of thieves, thugs and villains of all descriptions, the unmarried mother ranked as the lowest form of life. Such was the moral code of Victorian workhouse society.

There were stringent rules laid down by the workhouse guardians regarding the personal behaviour of the nursing staff. They were not allowed to talk to male staff unless under extremely urgent circumstances. Their living accommodation was nothing more than a tiny room with only the minimum essentials and was often referred to as the nurse's hutch: a small cupboard-like compartment with a bed and a small locker. They were forbidden to decorate their hutches or put up any pictures or ornaments. The reason given for this was that it inflicted extra cleaning duties on the already over-burdened cleaning staff. The nurses were forbidden to smoke, talk loudly or take part in improper conversation, and they had to be in bed asleep by 11 pm every night.

They had to work from 7.30 am to 8 pm six days a week with one half day off from 2 pm to 11pm. Even on their nights off they were still ordered to be in bed at 11 pm. The night duty was on a strict rota from 8 pm to 7.30 am and often one nurse had to manage up to thirty beds on her own, with many patients suffering from highly contagious diseases. In the poorer or smaller workhouses, the nurse did not even have her own separate accommodation but just bedded down in the ward along with her patients, and often the one nurse would be on duty day and night.

In the infirmaries conditions were slightly better, but there was still a desperate shortage of trained nurses. The First World War drained the country of nursing staff and was responsible for a complete upheaval of the system. The best of the infirmaries were taken over by the government to care for the war casualties. All of the patients from these institutions were transferred to neighbouring infirmaries which had at the same time to cope with the ever-increasing demand for beds and they had to take the overspill of civilian patients who would normally have been scheduled for admission to the war-casualty infirmaries. This put a tremendous pressure on the nurses who were already stretched to breaking point. Unlike the better organized and prestigious voluntary hospitals, the infirmaries could not refuse admittance to any patient needing hospital treatment. The voluntary hospitals could pick and choose their patients, but the over-worked infirmaries were left to cope with all the terminally ill, geriatric and imbecile patients, those cases being generally considered uninteresting by the voluntary hospital staff.

Also because the rates of pay and the general conditions of the voluntary hospitals were so much better than the infirmaries they attracted more highly trained nurses. These nurses would receive good food, properly cooked, and lived in comfortable staff quarters. This again reflected on the poorer standard of nursing staff in the infirmaries compared to the voluntary hospitals.

By 1913 nursing staff from the training hospitals could expect a wage of fourteen to nineteen shillings per week (equivalent to 70 pence to 95 pence per week), while the semi-trained nurses in the small country areas were only paid in the region of ten shillings per week (equivalent: 50 pence).

As time went on and the Welfare State system took over, the old workhouses gradually faded out of existence, and even the antiquated infirmaries were replaced by modern efficient hospitals as we know them. The life of a nurse became easier, though it has to be said that nurses' wages did not keep up with the ever-increasing national average.

It will be interesting to see if little Angela Mahony goes into the nursing profession when she grows up. At the moment she is too young to even think about what her future job might be, being only four years old. If she does become a nurse she will find herself living a very different lifestyle to that experienced by the nurses in the nine-teenth-century workhouses.

Angela is a very intelligent child and is very well behaved and seems to possess her own self-discipline, not usual in a child so young. She has been able to read and write from the age of three and has an awareness which surprises most adults.

Kathleen says, 'More than once, when I have been out shopping with Angie, people have stopped me in the street to remark on how old-fashioned Angie is. They always seem to wind up saying the same thing: "Oh, she's been here before".'

Angie's mother smiles to herself when she hears these remarks. She wonders what these strangers would think if they heard Angie's story about being a nurse in her previous life.

Young boy remembers being a German bomber pilot

Carl Edon, *Middlesbrough*

When young Carl Edon plays with his toy planes, his parents believe that it is not purely childish behaviour but is an action replay of the time when Carl remembers he was a pilot in the German Air Force.

'As soon as he could talk he used to tell us that he once crashed his plane into the windows of a building,' says his mother Valerie. 'We gather that he eventually died from multiple injuries sustained in the crash. We thought it strange that he should say such a thing, for as a tiny toddler he never showed any real interest in adventure stories and he had no time for looking at war films or such things.'

Valerie Edon went on to explain that as he grew older and started to gain more command over his speech the story became more detailed and he told it in such a matter-of-fact sort of way that she and her husband felt that they could no longer dismiss it out of hand as a little toddler's day-dream.

The incident which really persuaded the Edons that Carl's story had a ring of truth to it occurred when Carl first learnt to draw and to colour. Like most small children he went through the stage of experimenting with his coloured pencils and crayons and he had the usual colouring-in books and children's puzzle books in which he used to join up the dots to make a picture. One day he sat with his crayons and colouring-in book, but instead of colouring in the drawings, his mother noticed that he had drawn peculiar-looking badges and motifs all over the page.

The neatness of the drawing was the thing that most caught Valerie's attention. Unlike the normal scribbles of a three-year-old, Carl's little drawings were definite precise examples of various badges and insignia which Valerie confesses were completely foreign to her, except for one little drawing. There on the top corner of his colouring book Carl had drawn a perfect German swastika inside a circle, thus making it look like a badge. There were other small badges drawn with the expertise of a professional artist.

When Valerie questioned her son about the badges he replied, 'That's the kind of badges I wore on my uniform when I used to drive my plane.'

More surprises were in store when shortly after Carl's fifth birthday he drew the cockpit of his plane. He remembered the exact positions of all the various controls and he explained to his bewildered parents the function of each lever, dial and gauge. He even knew the location of the button which he remembers having to press in order to release the bombs.

Carl's father was intrigued with the amount of minute detail in his small son's drawings, particularly as he knew that Carl had never ever been in a plane of any description, and had certainly never been in a cockpit. 'I don't see how he could have got the information,' said his father. 'He certainly couldn't have got it from a picture book because he would have had to study the subject so thoroughly that we would have noticed, and in any case he did not possess any picture books containing German planes or cockpits.'

The little boy can remember how he enlisted in the Luftwaffe, the German Air Force, when he was nineteen years of age and he was stationed on a large air-force camp with a lot of huts in rows. Carl explains, 'The huts had sinks in them but no taps for the water. The water came out of a pump.' The boy recalls that he and his comrades were all trained in first aid and anyone who was injured was treated by the men themselves. All of them were called upon to perform this duty.

Valerie and her husband were taken aback when their young son suddenly told them that he had been made to salute a framed picture of Hitler. 'I couldn't believe my ears,' said Valerie. 'I had no idea that he ever knew, or had even heard of, the name Hitler. It certainly was never a topic of conversation at home.'

According to Carl, the troops were ordered to gather in a large assembly hall. He says, 'There was a picture of Hitler on the wall and we all had to stamp our feet and salute to this picture.' He can demonstrate the stamp and the salute, which he executes as if they were second nature to him.

In reply to his mother's question about what he wore when he was in the hall, he says, 'Grey trousers tucked into knee-high leather boots and a black jacket.' His parents did not really believe that what their son described was a proper German uniform, so without telling their child they went along to their local library and looked up some books, only to find that Carl had given a perfectly correct description of his uniform, badges, and the cockpit of his plane.

His parents were able to check even the smallest details of Carl's drawings against photographs which they found in an old book on German planes of the last war.

Carl can reconstruct in chilling detail his crash into the windows of the building. He was flying low over some buildings and he must have lost consciousness for a few moments: as he described things, 'It went all black for a moment.' When he came round in the cockpit of his plane he was aware of a building rushing towards him at great speed. He desperately wrenched at the controls in a frantic effort to avert the collision, but he was too late. The plane bulldozed its way right through the large glass windows of the building.

Carl remembers the horrendous sensation which swept over him as he realized that he had lost his right leg. The shock of the crash, and the loss of his limb, combined with his other injuries, affected him so severely that he died very shortly after the crash.

Sadly the fatal blow affected not only Carl, but a pretty

young fraulein from Carl's village back in Germany, to whom he was engaged to be married. They had been childhood sweethearts and had grown up together, although she was several years younger than he. He remembered his thoughts just before he died and how he felt great compassion for his young fiancée, knowing that she would ultimately be given the shattering news of his death. In Carl's typical understatement, 'I felt so sorry for her.'

Although Carl cannot recall much of what happened after he died, he is acutely aware of having had a younger brother who was also a pilot, and the strange thing is that he is convinced that this younger brother died shortly after he himself bled to death amongst the twisted debris of his wrecked plane.

He has clear memories of his father in his previous life, whose name was Fritz. Carl seems to have been very fond of the man, who appears to have been a jovial character. Carl says of him, 'He was so funny and always made me laugh, and he took me for nice walks in the woods.' He told Carl all about the trees and the flowers and plants that they would see on their rambles in the woods near their home in Germany. The village they lived in was picturesque, and nestled among hills and lush woodlands. 'It was not a very big place,' says Carl, 'but I liked it.'

His mother was the disciplinarian of the family and Carl remembers her as being small and plump with dark curly hair and smallish glasses which she used to wear on the end of her nose. 'She was a bit bossy,' says the boy, 'and I always had to do what I was told.'

He was made to do his share of the household tasks and he remembers that his regular chore was to gather the wood for the large open fires in their home. He has distinct memories of chopping up long tree trunks into small logs, then carting them home in his barrow to be stored as fuel. The smell of the newly-chopped logs made a vivid impression on the young boy. He describes it as

44

'a nice fresh smell which always reminds me of the woods.'

Other smells which linger in Carl's consciousness are those of cooking. He remembers how he used to be served a type of soup. 'It wasn't like the soup I get now,' he says. 'It was a dark red colour and was quite thick. My mother made it nearly every day.' Then Carl added with a laugh, 'I used to get other things to eat as well, only I can't remember what the other things were like. But I know I got them as well as the soup.'

Valerie Edon wonders if there could be any connection between Carl's memories of his past life, and other members of her family. She says, 'My sister-in-law is German by birth and her father was a German pilot during the last war.' She wonders if it is only coincidence that this man was also killed in action, being brought down by the British while he was at the controls of his plane.

While this sister-in-law was still a baby, her mother re-married an Englishman in Germany and then moved to England where the family have since settled. The baby was adopted by the English step-father. Valerie muses over the possibility that by some strange twist of fate, she has given birth to the child who was really meant for her sister-in-law to bear.

Valerie's other two children, Darren and Angela, are completely different from their brother Carl. Both are well built with dark hair and tan complexions, whereas Carl is of a slight build with pale blond hair and white eyelashes.

The Edons are still wondering why they felt compelled to call their little boy by the name of Carl. 'It is a most incredible thing,' says Valerie, 'because we decided to call him Carl not knowing that he would have any connections with Germany.'

At a visit to Carl's school on a parents' evening recently, Valerie spoke to Carl's teacher who said, 'He has strange eyes, and when I am talking to him about anything his eyes pierce straight through me.' The teacher went on to tell Valerie that if she gives Carl a sum to do, he gives her the correct answer in a flash. 'When I ask him how he worked it out, he just doesn't answer me. He seems to think that there is no need to bother working things out when he knows the answer already.'

Carl, now an extremely bright nine-year-old, has a perfectionist streak in him which belies his years. He is ultra precise in his manner, and is more than particular about his appearance and clothes. His mother takes great pains to have everything just so for him: the collars of his shirts must be beautifully ironed, and everything has to be scrupulously clean at all times. Could this possibly be a hangover from his strict military days?

'We had a visitor in for tea recently,' laughed Valerie, 'and Carl almost frightened the life out of her by solemnly describing in amazing detail all about Adolf Hitler, accompanied by goose-steps and salutes.

'As he gets older, though,' says Valerie, 'Carl doesn't say too much about his mysterious past life. It's as though he only remembers the odd flash every now and then.' His mother has noticed that he is not particularly interested in watching war films on television but when he does he sometimes points out a mistake in the German uniform. Once he pointed to an actor playing a German NCO and said, 'He is just like my sergeant.'

Perhaps the reason for Carl's lack of enthusiasm for war films could be that they remind him too much of the real thing. Who could blame him for not wanting to bring back to his conscious mind those horrific days of violence and death?

Girl remembers being her own great-grandmother

Kelly Williams, *Defen*

When Mrs Diane Williams was expecting her third child, the only cloud which overshadowed the happy coming event was the fact that the baby's great-grandmother, a gentle old lady called Nanny Wyatt, had just died, and sadly she would not see her new great-grandchild. She had passed away on 4 October, 1974, at the ripe old age of 89.

When baby Kelly was born on 4 May, 1975, Diane was acutely aware of a great sense of contentment and from that moment she ceased to mourn for her much-loved lost grandmother. Since then, after countless inexplicable incidents, Diane feels that her nan has returned to her in the form of her daughter Kelly.

It all started when Kelly was only two. One day she was sitting on her aunt Pam's lap when she turned to Pam and asked, 'Do you remember when you used to sit on my lap like this?' Both Diane and her sister Pam just laughed, thinking that the child was talking gibberish, but they were soon silenced when Kelly went on to describe how Pam used to wear her hair in a Cleopatra style, and added, 'And I used to comb it for you.'

Pam had indeed worn her hair in a straight sleek Cleopatra style, but that was twenty years earlier, when she was only four or five years old, and the person who used to comb it for her was Nanny Wyatt.

Kelly went on to tell the dumbfounded Pam that she remembered her freckled face, and then she asked Pam if she could please have the lovely red-and-white spotted dress because that was her favourite. Pam and Diane exchanged incredulous looks, as they realized that the dress to which Kelly was referring was one which Nanny

Wyatt had bought for Pam many years before. It was a fresh white cotton frock with red polka-dots on it and frills round the sleeves and neck.

How could Kelly possibly know anything about clothes long since discarded by her aunt? Her mother Diane admits that she was something of a non-believer before Kelly was born, but since the birth of her daughter she has completely reversed her opinions. 'I never believed in life after death or reincarnation,' says Diane, 'but since I have had Kelly I do believe. My husband Clive and I have become convinced that somehow Nanny Wyatt lives on – in our daughter. I know it sounds completely ridiculous, but Kelly actually speaks as if she really is Nanny Wyatt – as if she is one and the same person with the same store of memories.'

Clive has no explanation for Kelly's behaviour. 'It's just uncanny,' he says. 'Sometimes she leaves me feeling a bit creepy after listening to the things she comes out with.' Clive went on, 'I'm no expert on this kind of thing, but there's definitely something more to it than meets the eye.'

Pam in particular is awed by Kelly's remarks about things, places and events which took place years and years before the child was born. 'It was weird the way she described my dress and hairstyle, especially when she couldn't have seen a picture of me when I was young, because we just don't have one.' Another thing that puzzles Pam is the fact that the two-year-old referred to Pam's hairstyle as a 'Cleopatra' style. 'How did she know the style was called Cleopatra?' she asks. 'After all, that fashion is years out of date and the word Cleopatra has never been uttered by any of us in front of Kelly – there was just no reason to mention it.'

Diane noticed that even Kelly's speech and mannerisms were those of Nanny Wyatt. She says, 'Strangely, Kelly seems to know all about her great-grandmother, even though she has never asked me anything about the old lady. When she sits down in an armchair, she always fetches her toy handbag, and places it on the floor, tucked between one leg and the side of the chair, just like Nanny Wyatt used to. Most people would just plonk their handbags on the floor any old way, but not Nanny, or Kelly.'

Most of the people who knew the old lady, remark on the close similarity between Mrs Wyatt and Kelly. Diane says, 'Kelly is a neat and fussy little girl, exactly like my nan was. Like most little girls she loves to play with her dolls and handbags, but unlike most, the contents of her bag are always so neatly organized, with everything in the right compartment. Nanny Wyatt was constantly cleaning out and rearranging her handbag, so much so that it became almost an obsession with her. She could not bear a crumpled tissue or an odd sweet paper to clutter up her bag, and she would get really upset if she could not find a waste-paper bin instantly.'

'It is mystifying sometimes when Kelly talks about my grandmother,' says Diane, 'as she will refer to the old woman in the first person as if she was talking about herself. Then she will go on to relate things which happened before she was born and about which she could have no knowledge whatsoever.' Diane has noticed that her little girl has developed a fascination for fashions of the Victorian times, the clothes Nanny Wyatt would have worn when she was a young girl. 'Kelly can describe them all in great detail, talking about the clothes as "the clothes we wore then".' She seems to have definite objects in her mind which she will talk about every so often. Says Diane, 'There is a particular black dress which she has described so many times that I could almost run it up on my sewing machine.'

'My dress went right down to the ground,' insists Kelly, 'and it was black and the neck came right up to my chin. It had a white collar and long sleeves and the skirt could whirl out wide when I turned around quickly.'

Her parents just cannot understand where Kelly gets her information from. 'We have no books or pictures at home which could have told her so much,' says Clive. Then he added, 'Even if I came across any odd old papers or magazines containing photographs of Victorian times, I think I would be inclined to get rid of them straightaway, so that Kelly would not be influenced by them.' Diane says, 'Whenever I ask her where she gets so much information, she says that she used to watch the ladies in the ballroom and that she was peeping through the window and nobody saw her!' Diane is completely baffled by this and has not got the faintest idea of what her daughter means. 'The funny thing is,' laughed Diane, 'she never changes her story. No matter how I frame the question, she always comes out with the exact same answer: she was peeping through the ballroom window. As far as we are concerned ballrooms really are a thing of the past. In fact I don't think I've ever been in one in my life, so heaven knows where she gets it from.'

Some of Kelly's memories are connected with events which even her own mother had forgotten. Diane explains, 'One day Kelly told me that she enjoyed living in her little bungalow that time.' Diane is used to Kelly referring to herself as though she was Nanny Wyatt, so naturally she cast her mind back to see if she could remember her grandmother ever having lived in a bungalow. 'I was sure my grandmother had never lived in such a place, but Kelly kept on and on about it, even describing the curtains as being blue with little flowers. Then it suddenly came to me: Nanny had lived in a bungalow, but only for a few weeks and that was many years ago when I was just young myself. I had even visited her there.'

Diane's mother passed away suddenly on 13 March this year and left the whole family heartbroken. It was little Kelly who proved to be the strong one, and astounded the family by announcing, 'Nanny's at rest now with all the people she loved as much as us. She is with grandad Wyatt.' This summing up of the situation seemed to be coming from the lips of a much more mature person than a seven-year-old girl.

'She had a very special attachment to my mother, who

was Nanny Wyatt's daughter, of course,' says Diane. 'Mum had five grandchildren, including Kelly's brother and sister, Spencer, aged ten, and twelve-year-old Tracey, and they all used to play happily around her – except for Kelly. She used to mother my mum.'

On 12 June, Diane's sister got married and it was a very emotional occasion for the entire family, who were still grieving over the death of Kelly's grandmother. 'We are an extremely close family,' explains Diane, 'and at the wedding service, mum was sorely missed. We were all deeply upset because we knew how much she had been looking forward to the wedding.' Diane continued, 'There were a lot of tears in church. Kelly and my elder daughter were bridesmaids. She kept a firm eye on me and had such a courageous expression on her little face that I knew she was working overtime, willing me to smile and to keep up a brave front. I'll never forget the uncanny feeling I got when her eyes looked directly into mine. I got the distinct impression that if I broke down, I would be letting her down in some odd way. If it hadn't been for Kelly, I don't think I would have got through the service.'

Recently Diane was chatting to a friend about their teenage days. The two girls had been close companions at that time, but had somehow lost touch when Diane had become engaged to Clive. They became so engrossed in their reminiscences that they forgot for a moment that Kelly was sitting in the corner playing with her toys. Diane started to talk about a particularly enjoyable holiday she had had somewhere back in 1958 or 1959. Out of the blue, Kelly called out, 'Oh I remember it. That was the year we had the plague of ladybirds.'

Diane, who by this time had become quite used to Kelly's unexpected revelations just took the remark in her stride and acknowledged her small daughter's contribution to the discussion as being correct, but Diane's friend who was unaware of the child's extraordinary gift for accurately recalling past events, looked quite stunned as she asked Diane, 'Did you hear what she said?'

Diane laughed. 'Yes, she comes out with things like that from time to time.'

The friend was even more surprised at Diane's attitude of mild acceptance. She asked Diane, 'But how does she know about the ladybirds?'

Kelly's answer left her mother's friend totally perplexed. The little girl explained, 'I know it was the year of the ladybirds because when you went on that holiday to the seaside you wore that big funny hoop thing under your dress to make it stand out more, and your mother and I kept teasing you about it. Remember we called you a walking bell tent?'

Now it was Diane's turn to be left open-mouthed and speechless. She thought that by this time she had become shock-proof with Kelly, but this really took her unawares. Everything Kelly had said was true. It had been the late fifties when wide flouncy hula-hoop skirts with lots of frilly petticoats underneath were all the rage. Diane's mother did tease her, and the other person present at the time had been Nanny Wyatt.

Another insight into Kelly's peculiar sense of the past came to light when some members of the family were sitting in the lounge discussing the troubles in the Falklands. Someone expressed a fear that there might be some bombings on the British mainland, and immediately Kelly said, 'It was just the same during the last war, when they dropped the bombs. It was awful, and everyone knows Birmingham was badly hit during the war.'

'Nanny Wyatt's death was a great personal loss,' says Diane, 'but since Kelly began to demonstrate this inexplicable supernatural link with her, I have had a deep conviction that the old lady is still here.'

Kelly, now a chirpy seven-year-old, is a very self-confident child, perceptive and thoughtful, and she can hold a proper conversation with an adult as if she is on equal terms.

Girl remembers previous life in South Africa

Justine Shillito, *Reading*

One sunny summer afternoon when Justine was playing happily in the garden of her home in Reading, Berks, she turned to her mother and said, 'When I lived in Africa we had sunshine like this every day.'

As Justine was only three years old at the time and had never been out of England, her mother Beverly got quite a shock. Says Beverly, 'I went cold when she said this because I'd never read her any stories mentioning Africa and she never bothered to watch television apart from the odd children's programme.'

Beverly asked her daughter what her name had been when she lived in Africa and she was told Mary. As a test question, Beverly then asked Justine, 'Were the people black or white?' The child's answer confirmed her mother's suspicions that Justine's remarks were not just childish fantasy. Justine replied, 'Black poor ones and white ordinary ones.'

Over the course of the next few weeks Justine told her parents that when she lived in Africa she had two brothers and her mother had been called Ann. Her father had been a farmer of some type. They lived on a farm or a smallholding and they had lots of chickens and dogs.

Justine said that when she was Mary she did not go to school but just played around her house with a pet brown and white dog called Bimbo, which she fondly remembers. She is vividly aware of the climate being always dry and hot.

The family must have been reasonably well off because Justine says, 'We had our own pool in the garden and I went in it when I got very hot.' She remembers that her mother had domestic assistance and she described a Negro woman called Daisy who was 'very fat and black with lots

53

and lots of little woolly curls in her hair.' Justine says, 'Daisy helped my mummy and did the housework for her.'

Daisy lived with the family, but according to Justine the woman did not sleep in the main house but had her own quarters in a small hut at the end of the garden. There was also a black house-boy called Tom-Tom.

Daisy and Tom-Tom were most probably related in some way, possibly as husband and wife, or maybe as mother and son, because Daisy seemed to be very much in authority over Tom-Tom. According to Justine's memory, Daisy's word was law in the servants' quarters. Also Justine recalls just one wooden hut at the bottom of the garden, another factor which would indicate that the two servants were probably related.

Justine was very fond of Daisy but she had reservations about Tom-Tom. 'He stole my mummy's ring once,' said Justine. 'He pretended he didn't but Daisy found it in the hut.' Tom-Tom used to do the gardening, and help generally around the house. 'He liked to eat mealie,' says Justine. 'But I didn't like that, so Mummy never gave it to me.' Mealie is a slang term used to describe a meal of maize mixed with potatoes which is eaten by the natives of South Africa. This food was always eaten by Daisy and Tom-Tom in the wooden hut and never in the house.

Justine told her mother, 'The black people were over the other side.' This comment, together with the reference to the mealie suggests that Justine's former life may have been in South Africa.

Another point which bears this out is that Justine is absolutely petrified of what she calls 'baubies'. Her mother Beverly had no idea what a bauby was but she was alarmed at her little girl's fear which expressed itself each time the child raised the subject.

Beverly tried time and time to comfort her daughter but the fear of the terrible baubies caused the child to go into near hysterics. Beverly says, 'Each time I asked her what she meant by baubies she would just burst into tears with a look of absolute terror in her eyes.'

Unknown to Beverly or Justine, some research was carried out with the cooperation of South Africa House. At first there was no success whatsoever, and no one had even heard of anything called a bauby. It looked as if every avenue of investigation had been exhausted, and the terror that had menaced Justine's former life was destined to remain a mystery. As a final attempt to find an explanation, the question was put to a Negro employee at South Africa House who had spent many years living in the South African bush. She was asked, 'Have you ever heard of a bauby?' Immediately she replied, 'You mean *boerbee*? Of course. It's another name for Afrikaaner cattle.'

Boerbees are a particularly tough brand of cattle with extra-long, ferocious-looking horns, specially bred to survive in drought conditions. They are not like the normal docile cattle which we in the UK are accustomed to seeing grazing peacefully in our fields, but are left to roam wild, and appear to be extremely menacing. There would be every reason for a small girl to react with terror if she happened to find herself confronted with or attacked by a *boerbee*.

The words bauby and *boerbee* sound so alike, it is clearly possible that the child was referring to the latter word. This again would support the South Africa theory.

Another remark made by Justine which her mother did not understand was, 'I didn't get to go beside the kafas.' Beverly thought that Justine was talking about calves, because she had previously mentioned the fact that the family lived on a sort of farm, but the little girl said, 'No, not calves, Mummy. Kafas.' When Beverly asked her daughter what she meant by kafas Justine replied, 'You know, the black kafas.' Beverly didn't know that a kaffir is another word for a member of the South African Bantu and is also used in a wider context by white South Africans as a derogatory reference to any member of the Negro community. Perhaps what Justine meant to say was the word kaffir, which sounds so much like the little girl's word: kafa.

Beverly cannot understand how little Justine has such knowledge of a country and way of life which could not be more different from her lifestyle in Berks. The girl describes her garden in Africa with big fruit trees, the big swimming pool, and the large elegant white house with the flight of steps leading down to the pool, all in great detail.

'There were snakes in the garden sometimes,' recalls Justine, as she tells her mother how one day she was sitting with her mother when a snake appeared just inside the door which led directly out on to the back garden. She remembers that her mother was afraid and screamed to her father who was outside in the garden. The father rushed into the house carrying a huge boulder or heavy stone. 'He came in and saved us,' says Justine. She explains, 'Daddy hit the snake on the head with the big stone. Then he killed it.'

'Justine does not appear to be particularly frightened of snakes, at least no more so than anyone else,' says her mother, 'because although she said that her mother Ann had been afraid when the snake entered the kitchen, Justine made no mention of being afraid herself.' Beverly says, 'I'm sure that if she had experienced fear, it's the first thing she would have told me, especially since she mentioned the fact that her mother had been afraid. Perhaps she saw snakes quite regularly, or she may have been too small at the time to realize the danger, considering that she said that she did not go to school when she lived in Africa.'

The servants' hut at the bottom of the garden seemed to be out of bounds for Justine – or Mary as she was then called. 'Mummy told me I mustn't go down there,' the child remembers.

When Beverly was making an apple pie one day and Justine was watching her, supposed to be helping as all little girls like to do from time to time, the child said,

'That's not how Daisy made our pies.' When Beverly asked what was different about Daisy's pies, Justine replied, 'Daisy didn't cover them over on top like that. She just put lines over the apples.' 'She was obviously trying to describe an open tart,' said Beverly.

Justine told her mother that they had lots of apple trees in their garden and there was a big ladder which Tom-Tom used to climb up to collect the apples. It was also his job to spray the lawn and flowers with water using a long rubber hose-pipe. 'It was like a long snake,' says Justine.

Justine is sure that she had two brothers in her previous life in Africa but she does not recall their names or whether they were younger or older than herself. She remembers playing in the swimming pool with them and having fun being sprayed with the hose-pipe. Justine and her brothers used to gather the eggs from the chickens every morning and bring them to Daisy.

Justine's mother says, 'I often wonder what would happen if we ever took our little girl to South Africa. I wonder if she would be specially drawn to any particular part of the country. But I don't think we will manage such a trip in the foreseeable future.'

Maybe that's just as well for Justine's sake, when we remember her reaction to the Afrikaaner cattle. She is now a bubbling exuberant six-year-old who enjoys nothing more than tucking into her mother's English apple pie and fresh Devon cream.

Boy remembers being a garage mechanic

Jonathan Pike, *Leigh-on-Sea*

When Jonathan was three-and-a-half years old his parents moved from Hulbridge in Essex to the Priory Park area of Prittlewell on the outskirts of Southend-on-Sea. The first time his mother Anne took him out walking through the park little Jonathan had fun running through the thick carpet of red and rust-coloured leaves which had fallen from the trees. It was a glorious afternoon and the sun was streaming through the trees, highlighting the natural beauty of the autumn colours. There was a pleasant hint of burning wood in the air, and Anne noticed some men busy gathering up leaves and twigs into heaps to throw into a crackling brazier.

Jonathan turned to Anne and with a broad reminiscent smile on his face told her, 'When I was ten we used to come over here, and we set a bonfire alight and a policeman came and chased us away.'

Anne thought that the sight of the burning leaves had just set her little boy's imagination on a make-believe trip, making him think that he had been in the park before. She thought no more about the remark and didn't even tell her husband.

Some time later Anne was busy with her ironing. It was early evening and little Jonathan who was all ready for bed was watching her. He had been allowed to stay up just a little later than usual that evening, but as it was now well past his usual bedtime his father Tom decided that it was time to take his son upstairs and tuck him in for the night. After kissing his mother goodnight, Jonathan jumped up on his father's back piggy-back style and was taken upstairs. On the way up, the child said to his father, 'When I was a little boy the last time, my other mummy did ironing.' Tom was mildly surprised to hear this, but he didn't over-react. He remembers, 'At first I thought that I must have heard the wrong thing, or that he had got a bit jumbled up in what he was trying to say.'

Tom asked Jonathan, 'You mean you've been watching mummy do the ironing.' The child replied, 'Not this mummy, my other mummy.' His father asked him, 'What other mummy?' Jonathan replied, 'The one that I had when I was here before.' Tom says, 'He seemed so definite that it made me wonder, so I asked him what he meant when he had said that he'd been here before.' Jonathan told his father, 'I used to live near here before when I was a little boy the last time with my other mummy and daddy.'

Because Tom had never heard Jonathan say anything vaguely like that before, he really began to feel uneasy. He says, 'I put him into his bed, and I remember feeling very odd. I looked at him lying there relaxed and smiling away as if he'd said something quite ordinary and normal. I could see that he wasn't in the least bothered by having been here before.' Tom then tucked his little boy in and kissed him goodnight. Just as he got to the bedroom door, Jonathan called to his father, 'Daddy, when my other mummy did her ironing she showed me how to put creases in my trousers.'

A bewildered Tom made his way back downstairs to join his wife. He told Anne all about what Jonathan had been saying and then she told him about the child's remarks in the park about having been there before when he was ten.

Jonathan's parents could well imagine how a little boy might make a remark about a bonfire, and that he had been watching ironing, but the one thing they couldn't fathom was how Jonathan could know anything about putting creases in trousers. Tom usually wears jeans around the house and any time his trousers need to be pressed they are sent to the dry cleaners. Anne says, 'I wouldn't even attempt to press his good trousers in case I made a mess of them.' She has never ever pressed creases in trousers and Jonathan, being only three years old, had always worn children's permanently pressed trousers. Anne says, 'All the kids' trousers nowadays come either permanently creased, or else like his little shorts with no creases in them at all.' They were surprised that Jonathan even knew what the word crease meant.

Shortly after that Anne took Jonathan out on a bus past some very large white houses in Chalkwell. Suddenly Jonathan pointed over to the houses and said, 'That's where Angela lived.' Anne asked him who Angela was and he replied, 'She was my wife.' Anne couldn't believe her ears. She said to Jonathan, 'How could you have a wife? You're only three.' Jonathan answered, 'Yes, but when I was here the last time I grew up into a big man and Angela was my wife.'

The child then went on to say that when he had been living before, he had had a son and daughter and the little girl was also called Angela after her mother. Jonathan remembered that his little girl had lots of long curls in her hair and she used to have them tied at each side with ribbons. This seemed to stick in his mind. He told Anne that before little Angela would be put to bed his wife used to brush the child's hair and put what he described as long cloth bandages in her hair. He went on to explain that in the morning when the bandages would be taken off, Angela's hair would be all covered in long curls.

Later that same day when Anne was returning on the bus by the same route, they travelled down Chalkwell Avenue and when they came to the crossroads where Crosby Road crosses the Ridgeway, Jonathan became very agitated and he looked very upset. Anne was watching him but she didn't say anything. He suddenly turned to her and said, 'That's where my little girl got killed.' Anne says, 'He looked really sad and I thought he was going to cry. I asked him if he was all right and he nodded and then said, "My little girl Angela got killed by a car there."'

After that first bus journey Jonathan always said the

same thing about his little girl being killed and each time they would go down that road on the bus he always pointed to the same spot by the crossroads. He never once changed his mind or got confused about this. He remembered that little Angela had run out on to the road and a car had run over her, killing her outright.

On another occasion, again when they were on a bus travelling between the Bell Public House and Cuckoo Corner, Jonathan pointed to a big garage called Earl's Hall Motors and said, 'That's where I used to work as a mechanic.' He told his mother that he had to fix all the cars and that he knew how to fit engines.

Jonathan has two smaller sisters, Elizabeth and Louise, and one day when Anne was bathing the girls, Jonathan said to her, 'I used to bath Angela like that.' His little sisters were one and two at the time, and Elizabeth, the two-year-old, asked Jonathan who Angela was. Then she giggled. 'Is she your dollie?' she asked. Jonathan became quite indignant at this question and in a superior manly voice he informed his little sister, 'I didn't have dollies. Angela was my daughter.' Of course Elizabeth didn't know what her brother was talking about and just splashed about merrily in her bath, but Anne understood what he meant. She said to Jonathan, 'Did you really have a little girl called Angela?' He replied firmly, 'Yes, and she got killed.' Anne then asked him, 'What about your little boy?' Jonathan said, 'I can't remember what his name was. I only remember Angela's name because it was the same as my wife's.'

Jonathan told his mother that when he was married to Angela he went to live in the Chalkwell area in one of the big white houses. He said that he had a nice big garden and he used to grow lots of flowers and vegetables. He couldn't remember the actual address or number of the house but he was certain that it was somewhere in Chalkwell.

Because the family had only just moved to the area, Anne cannot understand how Jonathan knew the name

61

Chalkwell, where it was, or that such a place even existed. They were totally new to the entire district and Jonathan had never been taken to Chalkwell apart from the times when he was on the bus with his mother.

Although there are four garages in the area, three are simply filling stations. Earl's Hall Motors, the oldest garage in the area, is the only one where mechanics were employed. Because Jonathan cannot remember his previous name it is difficult to check back to see if there ever was a mechanic employed there who would fit the description of the man Jonathan thinks he used to be.

The main lead was the fact that his little girl had been killed in a road accident at the crossroads on Chalkwell Avenue. There is no one living in the area at present who can recall an accident at that spot involving a small girl called Angela, but again because there is no surname people find it difficult to think back. Very often when a small child is knocked down and killed on the road, the people will remember the incident according to the family name, as it were, the Jones girl, or Billy Smith's daughter. They would not necessarily remember the child's Christian name.

Prior to 1960 the Southend police were an independent force but then they merged with the county police and all the old records from the Southend station have been stored away in vaults. Again, in the absence of a date or surname, it would be an almost impossible task to try to dig up details of such a fatal accident. However, a long-serving police officer, Sergeant Ernie Dark of Southend Traffic Police, does remember a fatal accident involving a child at that very spot some thirty years ago, and he recollects that the child who was killed was a little girl.

Two-year-old girl remembers being a mother

Gaynor Marsh, *Isle of Man*

When Mrs Margery Marsh, a busy mother with two children, ran out of the family's favourite breakfast cereal, she decided to give the children porridge, hoping that they would find it a pleasant change from their usual morning fare.

Seven-year-old Laurie who was rushing to get ready for school made little comment on the change of menu, but his two-year-old sister Gaynor was quite nonplussed about having to eat porridge.

'I don't like porridge,' she told her mother.

'How do you know you don't like it?' asked her mother. 'You've never had it before.'

'Oh yes I have,' insisted Gaynor. 'When I was a little girl before I had it and I didn't like it then either.'

The harassed mother sighed, although she couldn't help smiling to herself as she heard Gaynor's remarks about when she was a little girl before. Margery assumed that this was just a trumped-up argument against having to eat porridge, and she marvelled at the ingenuity of it. 'I certainly hadn't heard that one before,' says Margery, 'but I just thought it was Gaynor's imagination providing her with an excuse not to eat breakfast, so I didn't pay too much attention to it, and in fact I didn't even comment on her words.'

Gaynor's mother tried to convince her that she could not possibly know whether or not she liked the porridge until she had tasted it. Margery suggested that perhaps if she added some raspberry jam it would brighten up the meal, which she admitted didn't look all that enticing. In spite of her mother's efforts, Gaynor was adamant. She didn't like porridge and that was that. She then turned tearfully to her mother and remarked, 'When I was a mummy I didn't make my little girls eat things they didn't like.'

'What little girls?' snapped Margery impatiently as she reluctantly threw Gaynor's porridge in the bin. Her daughter answered, 'My two little girls, when I was a mummy.' She added, 'And I didn't shout at them. When I was a mummy I was nice to my little girls.'

Margery did not know what to think of her child's remarks, but over the following weeks and months the story of Gaynor's two little girls did not alter. Gaynor remembered how she used to play with the little girls and how she used to teach them to sew and how to make things. She said that she only gave them the things to eat which they liked and that the one special treat that the girls loved was when she took them out to pick black-berries and they got to eat some on the way home. She used to let the girls watch her make jam with the berries but she wouldn't let them stir the jam when it was hot in case they got their fingers burnt, although she did allow them to help her prepare the fruit.

Gaynor used to make unprompted comments about what her girls used to do and how they all got on together and what they looked like. Gaynor remembers them as having 'nice long frocks right down to the ground'.

'It's funny,' says Gaynor's mother. 'Every time I used to ask her any questions about her little girls she would never answer me. I didn't press the questioning. I realized that if I asked her any specific question it might put the idea into her head and give her some material upon which to build, so I purposely kept off the subject.'

Gaynor's mother feels that the memories were sparked off by various happenings in everyday life. For example, when the child was offered porridge for breakfast it reminded her of how she had disliked porridge in her previous life. She says, 'She seems to have been very close to her daughters.'

Before all this developed, something very odd happened. For the first time Gaynor managed to say a complete sentence. It was shortly after her second birthday. Her mother recalls, 'We were out for a walk one afternoon, and I decided to take Gaynor along a narrow country road where she had never been before, just for a change of scenery.' As they ambled down the road, they came to an old cemetery. 'Immediately Gaynor set eyes on the graveyard she got very excited,' says Margery. 'At first I thought it was something to do with the flowers which had been left at the various tombstones, but I soon realized that the flowers had nothing to do with Gaynor's reaction. She kept jumping up and down and pointing towards the cemetery. Then to my amazement she yelled out her first complete sentence: "That is where I was born."

'The words hit me in an odd way,' says Margery. 'There was something in her tone – a sort of conviction, which left me stunned. She had never ever said a complete sentence like that before, just the usual baby talk, and it struck me as very strange that she should choose such unusual words with which to make her break-through. I got such a shock that I couldn't get away from the cemetery quick enough.'

When Gaynor was only a few months old, Margery had had an unforgettable experience which left her convinced that she had been given a glimpse of the past. In view of Gaynor's remarks about a previous life, Margery feels that what she saw could be linked up with her daughter's past.

'We had gone to bed, and baby Gaynor was fast asleep in her crib in the corner of our bedroom,' says Margery. She goes on to explain that she suddenly found herself in the doorway of a room totally unknown to her. She could see into the room which was illuminated by a pinkish orange light, and there inside was a family she had never seen before in her life – a father, mother, and two or three young children.

'The first thing that impressed me,' says Margery, 'was the fact that they were all wearing very old-fashioned clothes. They were simple and looked as though they had been hand-made.' Margery remembers that the woman's ankle-length dress was of a coarse type of deep brown linen or cotton and was perfectly plain. It was gathered at the neckline and waist by some type of cord or rope, and there was a long white apron over the dress, like an old-fashioned pinafore.

The father sat by a great blazing fire and the children were playing on the floor. Margery was aware of the children laughing and talking but she could not make out what was being said; in fact she is not sure whether she actually heard any sounds or not, and she feels that she received more of an impression of laughter and sound rather than actually hearing it.

The room was sparsely furnished, giving the impression that the family must have been rather poor. The bits and pieces of furniture were very crude, and like the clothes, they too seemed to have been home-made. There was a large wooden table, a couple of rough-looking wooden benches. The father sat on one of the benches smoking a peculiar-looking pipe with an extra long stem. Margery recalls that she was puzzled about the pipe because it was not a type usually seen in England. She says, 'It was more of a Continental pipe, like the ones you see in Holland.'

The man wore a lightish coloured shirt and a dark brown jacket. Margery could not see his face because he had his hand up to it as he held the pipe.

'I got the feeling of the 17th century, for some reason,' says Margery, 'and although the family seemed to be poor, it was not abject poverty, and I think they probably managed to get by O.K.' As Margery stood in the doorway watching the family, she expected them to notice her and ask her what she wanted. She says, 'The strange thing was they didn't pay the slightest bit of attention to me. They just acted as if I wasn't there.'

Margery felt herself strongly drawn towards the mother. 'I just couldn't take my eyes off the woman,' she explains. 'The mother was setting a meal out on the big table, using wooden plates and bowls and very large coarse-looking wooden platters. She was standing with her back to the fire, facing the table and I could distinctly see that she must have been in her twenties. Her hair was tied back from her face and she wore a little scarf or kerchief on her head, tied back behind her neck and underneath her hair. I was looking at a side view of the woman,' says Margery, 'and I could see that her apron hung loosely from her shoulders, and she had her sleeves rolled up as she worked with the food.'

Suddenly Margery felt herself being pulled backwards, but she was still unable to take her eyes off the woman. The doorway became smaller and smaller until it looked like a black tunnel, then it seemed like a small black hole and she realized that she was looking into the pupil of an eye. She then became aware of the fact that the eye was that of her baby daughter Gaynor, who was quietly lying in her cot.

For a moment Margery stood looking at the baby, then she turned away from the cot to go back to bed. She became petrified with fear when she saw herself lying in the bed fast asleep beside her husband. 'I'll never forget how afraid I felt at that moment,' says Margery. 'The next thing I knew, I was awake, sitting up in bed looking around me. I think the shock woke me up.'

Margery had had what is known as an out-of-the-body experience, known as O.O.B.E. for short, in which her etheric or astral body separated from her physical body during sleep. Her entire consciousness and personality were present with her ego in the etheric body, leaving the physical shell housing only the material components – flesh, bones, blood, etc. The physical body still continues to function normally during an O.O.B.E. but at a very subdued level, i.e. the heart still beats, the blood continues to circulate, but these things happen automatically, rather like when an aeroplane is flying on automatic pilot.

Margery believes that the scene she witnessed actually took place in her daughter Gaynor's previous life. She feels that Gaynor was the mother of the family – the woman to whom Margery felt inexplicably drawn, and she feels that the children playing on the floor were in fact the little girls that Gaynor constantly referred to. She is almost certain that there were three of them ranging in age from two to five. Although she could not see them clearly she has the strong impression that they were Gaynor's daughters.

The interesting point about this is that Margery's out-of-the-body experience happened when Gaynor was only four months old, long before the child started to relate her memories of her previous life. So the scene which Margery witnessed could not possibly have been implanted in her mind by any of Gaynor's comments. She sums up the experience as, 'almost as if I had been inside my daughter and was able to tune into her past'.

For a long time Gaynor used to talk to two invisible friends. Her mother often heard the child engrossed in conversation in her bed at night. 'I could only, of course, hear a one-way conversation,' says Margery, 'but it always seemed to follow a logical format. It wasn't just a string of random ideas or words. The things she said seemed to tie up with inaudible questions and answers. It appeared as if she really was talking to people in the room unseen by me but apparently quite visible to her. I would watch her expressions and her eye movements and it seemed as if she was focusing on someone while she directed her speech to that particular area'.

Whenever Margery asked Gaynor who she was speaking to she would only reply, 'Just my lady and gentleman.' The child would never volunteer any further information, and Margery thought it wise not to question her on the matter.

One of Gaynor's oddest remarks came when she was sitting on her brother Laurie's knee. She said, 'I'm sitting on my daughter's friend's knee.' Margery thinks that this remark indicates that the family were all known to each other, or even related, in some previous life.

Margery had suffered a miscarriage before Gaynor was

born but when she was carrying her daughter, she had a strange dream in which she clearly saw the baby that was in her womb. She remembers the little face and how the child seemed to speed forward in time. One moment she was holding a tiny new-born baby with not a hair on her head and the next moment the child leapt down from Margery's arms and started to run about. The face of the child in the dream was identical to the face of Gaynor when she was born, and again when she developed into a toddler. Margery was so impressed by the dream that she told her husband that she was sure that this time she would not have a miscarriage and that the baby would be born. She described the baby in her dream to her husband, telling him that she was convinced that she had been shown the baby waiting to be born. In the dream Margery thought that Gaynor was one of twins. She did not have twins when her daughter was born, but some time later she was diagnosed as expecting twins, though sadly she suffered a miscarriage and lost them. She is certain that Gaynor was meant to be born to her in response to some long-forgotten link between them in the past.

Boy remembers being in his aunt's womb

Desmond Sanderson, *Coventry*

Three-and-a-half-year-old Desmond was playing on the floor with his toy cars one day when completely out of the blue he looked up at his mother Dorothy and said, 'You know, Mummy, I went to Aunty Ruth before I came to you, but I didn't stay there very long.'

The words made Dorothy stop in her tracks because her sister-in-law Ruth, the Aunty referred to by Desmond, had given birth to a still-born son almost ten years previously.

Dorothy says that her sister-in-law suffered a double tragedy because shortly after she lost her baby, her husband was killed in an accident. Dorothy says, 'It was all too much for poor Ruth and she almost had a nervous breakdown. It took her a long time to recover, but she has never been able to talk about her baby or her husband. As a mark of respect, the rest of the family took their cue from Ruth and to this day no one has ever mentioned either the baby or the husband.

'That is why I am absolutely certain that my small son could never have heard about the dead baby, let alone interpret it in the way he did,' explains Dorothy.

As his mother listened quietly, little Desmond told her that he remembered everything quite clearly, and that he was very warm when he was with Aunty Ruth. 'It was quite bouncy,' he said, 'and I used to turn round and round all the time.'

He remembered feeling very happy and comfortable and very wet. It was always dark but it didn't frighten Desmond. It all seemed perfectly natural. He used to get sleepy sometimes, and said, 'One time I just went to sleep but when I woke up again I wasn't with Aunty Ruth any more.'

His mother asked him where he was then. His reply surprised her: 'I went back home, of course.' Dorothy laughed. 'He said it in such a tone of voice that it made me feel quite foolish, as if I should have known that he went home – wherever that was!'

When his mother asked him where his home was, Desmond said, 'The place that I lived in before I went to Aunty Ruth, where all the nice fields are, and all the other little boys and girls. I went back to Robert and Samantha.'

Over the following weeks Dorothy heard more of her son's story of how he had special friends at home before he went to his Aunt Ruth called Robert and Samantha, and that there were also bigger people who looked after the children. He described how all the children were together and that they played lots of games.

The games were sometimes organized as in the case of the boat races which the child described, but mostly the children just played at what they liked. The boat races were evidently part of some type of gala or celebration, because Desmond was aware of dressing in a special robe for the occasion. He described taking part in a regatta with Samantha and Robert. He was in the same boat as Robert, but Samantha was with some of her other friends in another boat. There were lots of decorations on the boats – mostly flowers. He said that it was easy to make the boats go, but they didn't have any sails because there was no wind.

'On holidays we all had to sing,' said Desmond. He told how sometimes they got important visitors who came to play music for them. Desmond said that he never got any sweets in his other home but he remembered eating fruit. 'It was juicy and nice,' he said, and went on to describe what his mother thought must have been some kind of plum but bigger, and with no stone in the centre. He made an odd remark about the fruit when he told his mother, 'Some of the sick people got fruit to make them better after they died.'

There were pets in Desmond's home, and many of the

children played with rabbits and dogs. He was friends with a tiny green and yellow bird which used to accompany him everywhere. The bird always stayed with him.

It is interesting to note that there was some continuity in Desmond's story regarding the period which was spent waiting to be born in his aunt's womb. 'I didn't like to question him too closely,' says Dorothy, 'but it seems that somehow he remembers some of the incidents as having happened before he went to his Aunty Ruth, and some afterwards. I mean after he left Ruth and before he came to me, although there does seem to be some mix-up regarding time. I get the feeling that the time element in Desmond's previous life is not based on the same principles as our earthly time. He seems to have some difficulty sorting out exactly when the various incidents occurred, but he is in no doubt as to the reality of his experiences.'

The fact which suggests that there is some continuity in the chain of events remembered by Desmond is that he vividly remembers saying goodbye to his pet bird before he left his home to go to his Aunt Ruth. He then had an awareness of being in the womb and he seemed to know the identity of his mother at that time. Then after falling into a sleep he remembers going home again, and then he remembers meeting his little green and yellow bird – the same bird to which he had said goodbye before.

This also seems to suggest that the conception of Desmond in Ruth's womb was a carefully planned affair. He was well advised of what was about to happen to him and he prepared for a parting from his friends and his pet bird. Desmond also seemed to be aware of being called away from his permanent home when it was time for him to go to his present mother. He said, 'I knew I was coming to you and Daddy, because they told me.' This would strongly suggest that nothing happens by chance.

According to Desmond, there was something very special about the water at his other home. Says Dorothy, 'He told me about how the children used to play in pools of water, but when I asked him if he went swimming he said no. Then I asked him if he meant that he had gone paddling in the water the way he does now. Again he said no. I thought at that point that he was just playing me up, but when I heard his next remark I realized that there must be something more to it.'

Desmond's explanation of the water was, 'We didn't have to swim because we didn't sink and we never got wet.' He went on to tell his mother that when he went into the water with his friends they used to float on top of the water which seemed to support them and the drops of water just fell off them when they got out of the pool. 'Sometimes we went underneath the water,' said Desmond, 'but it didn't go in my mouth or in my eyes.'

'The most incredible thing of all,' says Dorothy, 'is that Desmond told me that the water made some sort of sound – like music.' Her son had said, 'The water played songs for us, Mummy, but not with words in them. When we picked up some water it went tinkle tinkle.' Desmond said that as well as sounds, the water had colours in it 'like little rainbows, but sometimes just one colour at a time.' The water was described as being soft to the touch and did not penetrate clothes or objects. It just seemed to bounce off in drops and made its own way back to the pool. 'When we got out of the water we were all dry straightaway without towels,' said Desmond, as if it was the most natural thing in the world.

Another time Desmond suddenly said, 'I've been to school, Mummy.' At that time the child had just started to attend play-school so of course Dorothy thought that Desmond was referring to that. She made some casual answer about hoping that he liked his play-school, but then he said, 'No, I mean the big children's school when I was at home with all my friends.'

Desmond related his story about how the children attended school and were taught lots of things. The teachers also looked after the children as guardians and all of them lived at the school. 'It seems that it was like a kind of school village,' says Dorothy. 'Not exactly a boarding school and certainly not as strict. The way Desmond describes it it appears almost like a holiday-camp with lessons thrown in.'

'He cannot remember the things he was taught,' says Desmond's mother, 'but he seems to know that there were lots of books. It's funny, but although Desmond is something of a tear-away little fellow he does have a great respect for books. I belong to a book club myself and I treasure my books very much, yet I feel quite confident when Desmond looks at them. I know that he wouldn't dream of tearing them or scribbling on them. He can't read, of course, but he enjoys looking through the books. Sometimes I have to laugh at his serious expression as he looks up and down the printed pages. I often wonder what is going on in his mind.'

Dorothy has never told Ruth about Desmond's remarks because more and more she is becoming convinced that her little boy must have been the child Ruth was expecting.

'She has no children of her own at all,' explains Dorothy, 'so I am afraid to tell her about Desmond in case she feels that he really belongs to her. In any case, I couldn't bear to start digging up the past again. Ruth has come to terms with her circumstances and it would be unfair and cruel of me to remind her of what she obviously would prefer to forget.'

As Desmond gets older the stories of his other home become fewer and fewer. 'Now that he's six he seems to have forgotten most of it,' says his mother, 'but every now and then he comes out with some odd remark which leaves me puzzled.'

Apart from these remote flashes, the last complete incident to be related by Desmond was when he was almost five. 'We were in the garden at the time,' says Dorothy, 'and I was showing Desmond how to plant some flower seeds. He took my breath away when he told me he used to make his own singing flowers when he lived with his friends.'

When his mother asked him what he meant by singing

flowers he replied, 'You know, the flowers with the music coming out of them.' It seems that Desmond and one of his friends had been taught how to make flowers by some man who knew all about them. He was taught that all he had to do was to think of the flower, stage by stage, and the flower would appear. Apparently the stem would materialize, followed by the leaves and petals, etc., and the colour of the flower would correspond to the colour willed by Desmond. If he wanted a pink flower it would become pink. 'The shapes of the flowers were different to the ones in our garden,' said the child.

'Like the water, these flowers had some kind of sound attributed to them,' says Dorothy. Seemingly, after the flowers were completed, some kind of force instilled itself into them and came from the petals in the form of sound or music. 'I may have some of it wrong,' says Dorothy, 'but that's the way I can describe it from what Desmond has told me. I know the whole thing sounds too ridiculous for words, but for that very reason, I am certain Desmond must have had some strange experiences.' Then Dorothy added with a laugh, 'He's certainly never seen musical flowers in our garden. We're lucky if we manage a few dandelions.'

Desmond's father John is taking his son's remarks seriously. He says, 'We don't really discuss it much, especially since he's started school, because the kid seems to have forgotten most of it now – at least he never mentions much about his other life. But at the time I remember thinking that there was no way that a youngster of his age could possibly have such things in his head unless he had lived through it all. It's not just the stuff about the water and the flowers,' says Desmond's father, 'but how he could tell us that he went to his Aunt Ruth before he came to us is unbelievable. If she had never lost a baby, then it would be different, but that one fact casts a whole new light on the matter. There's no doubt in my mind that the kid must have experienced life beforehand

and those memories stayed with him during his first three or four years on the Earth.'

Going to school was the turning point for Desmond, as that was the period when the memories seemed to fade into the background and the stories all but ceased, apart from occasional isolated remarks. Possibly the reason for this could be that when he went to school, the child had to absorb an increased amount of knowledge, facts and figures at a comparatively accelerated pace, and his brain was too busy dealing with this new information to allow the older memories to manifest themselves.

Girl remembers being lady of the manor

Gayle Woodward, *Liverpool*

Since Gayle Woodward was only two she has had a very advanced vocabulary for her age. Her mother Edna describes Gayle as petite and fairy-like, and a little old-fashioned in her ways.

The family always ate lunch in the kitchen and one day when they had just finished eating, Gayle said, 'I will have my coffee in the lounge, please, Mummy.' Gayle's father was tickled at this remark from his two-year-old, and jokingly asked her, 'What were you before, Gayle, a lady?' To the surprise of her parents, the child replied, 'Yes of course, why?'

Edna then asked Gayle what made her think that she had been a lady. Gayle replied, 'When I lived at the big house with all the rooms I was a lady.' When her mother asked her what house she meant, Gayle said, 'The big house with lots of steps going down from the door. The one with the big rooms and tall roofs, remember?' Gayle's mother told her that she didn't know any big house like that, but the child insisted that she used to live in the house, saying, 'It was when I was a big lady and I used to wear my pretty long dresses.'

Edna knew that Gayle had never visited or known about such a house, but she and her husband listened while Gayle described her memories of her former life. She said that there were lots of people at the big house who did all the work, and there was a man whose job it was to carry the bags. There were several horses, some of which were used to pull a coach which belonged to her family.

Gayle remembers how the coach was always kept in shining condition. She says, 'One of the helpers used to keep polishing it to keep the lanterns shiny.' She describes the coach as being black with lanterns on each side. There was one seat inside the coach and there was a high seat up on the top at the front where the man used to sit 'to drive the horses'. Gayle distinctly remembers lots of brasswork on the coach, which was always gleaming. 'The inside seat was red,' she says, 'and there was red on the inside of the doors at the bottom, but at the top of the doors it was glass, just like the windows.'

She remembers that sometimes one horse was used to pull the coach and sometimes two. She says, 'But Gypsy never went in front of the coach, only some of the other horses. Gypsy was my special horse and he was lovely.'

The coach was used by the family all the time, and Gayle says, 'Sometimes it would be sent to collect people who wanted to come to visit us at our house, especially when we used to have the big parties.' Gayle remembers that her family did a lot of entertaining, but she does not remember specific members of her family. She seems only to be aware of the fact that she lived in the big house as part of the family, and that there were lots of people around. 'It's more the lifestyle that she remembers,' says her mother, 'rather than individual relatives.'

'I liked it when we had the big parties because I got to wear my best dresses,' recalls Gayle. She described her dresses as being long with lots and lots of frills on them and little ribbons and bows on the sleeves. 'I had lots of pretty dresses in different colours and they all had big fat bits at the back,' says the little girl.

It would seem that Gayle was describing a bustle which was very much in fashion in the eighteenth century. She describes how they had a very large room where all the guests would gather. She explains, 'We always had dancing and there were men who played music.' Gayle says that the dancing took place after all the food and tables were cleared away so that there was plenty of space. 'There were lots of men with funny jackets on with big long bits down the back, and they had sticking up collars and fancy ties like butterflies.'

There was one particular horse, Gypsy, which Gayle

was very attached to. One day she asked her mother if she could have another horse just like Gypsy. Her mother thought at first that she was talking about her rocking horse and she asked the child why she needed another one. Gayle replied, 'Not Rocky. I mean my other horse that I had at the big house.' Rocky is the name Gayle gives to her rocking horse. She described Gypsy as being 'very big and black and I used to go on his back'.

Edna says, 'At first we thought that she had a lively imagination, but she described everything so fully that her father and I began to wonder. She was so emphatic about the big house and the horse that we felt sure that she must have had some kind of experience to match her story. She only watches children's programmes on television and we are sure that she could not have picked up so much detail from the television. We now believe that she has lived on this Earth before. Each time she mentions anything to do with the big house she always ends up with the same thing: "And I always used to have my coffee in the lounge." '

Gayle has shown a great fascination for old-fashioned jewellery and she loves the ballet. She has started to hoard things, especially old brooches, and she has quite a collection now, built up mainly through going to jumble sales.

Once Edna thought she would give Gayle a new hairstyle, but as soon as she produced the scissors to start clipping, the little girl adamantly refused to have her hair cut. She told Edna, 'I like it long the way I always used to have it when I was a big lady.' Gayle told her mother that when she was a lady her hair was very long and she never had to brush it herself. She had a special maid – or helper, as she put it – who used to look after her and take care of her clothes. The maid always brushed her hair for her and put it in curls with 'a funny hot stick thing' – Gayle's words for curling tongs. She wore a variety of hats and these were kept in pretty boxes, which her maid looked after. She remembers a little black hat which she only wore when she went riding on Gypsy.

'Sometimes my helper put other hair on top of my head,' remarks Gayle. 'It was white, not like my own hair.' This other hair which Gayle refers to would seem to be a powdered wig such as was worn by eighteenth century ladies of high rank.

Gayle is very demure and ladylike and has a sense of dignity which is highly unusual for such a small child. She accepts her previous life as part of her background which to her appears perfectly natural, as if everyone has lived before.

Says Edna, 'She takes the whole thing so for granted, she seems to know that there is nothing extraordinary in remembering her past life. I think she assumes that we have all been here before.'

Perhaps Gayle is right and we do have memories of our previous lives buried deep down in our subconscious minds, just waiting to be sparked off by some key word or experience which acts as a trigger to release the flood of memories.

Girl remembers being a witch

Julie Tomlinson, *Dagenham*

Long before little Julie reached her second birthday she was able to produce very distinctive drawings, not of flowers or houses or any of the usual efforts of a tiny child, but very elaborate detailed sketches, always on the same subject: witches!

Julie's grandmother was so intrigued by watching the child feverishly drawing what looked suspiciously like a witch one day, that she asked, 'What is that you're drawing, Julie?' The answer was more than Granny had bargained for, 'It's me of course, when I used to be a witch.'

Mrs Tomlinson just stared at the child in disbelief, wondering where on earth she had got the word witch from. It was certainly not the kind of thing anyone in the family ever discussed, and since Julie was not even two years old she couldn't have read about witches anywhere. Julie could never have heard the word at home because her parents don't like that sort of thing. In fact Julie's mother is a bit wary of anything she doesn't understand, and witches definitely come into that category.

One of the strangest things about Julie's drawings is the speed at which she can complete them. Her grandmother says, 'Ever since she has been able to hold a pen in her hand she has been drawing the witches. She completes a picture so fast it's almost as if she doesn't have to think about what she is doing. It all comes out sort of automatically, but despite the speed, she still manages to put in a wealth of detail. It's really uncanny for someone so young.'

Julie's drawings follow a distinctive style – full of individuality and not like the rough scribbles of other children of her age. She has a peculiar way of drawing the people in the background of her pictures. They seem to be done more in some type of symbol language than as straightforward sketching. Also the trees and flowers are done in the same manner. Mrs Tomlinson explains, 'They are always queer shapes, more as if they are meant to represent the trees and flowers rather than actually picture them as they look.'

Although the background material to Julie's pictures is in symbol form, there is no mistaking the main subject of the drawings. The witches are drawn fully and in perfect detail. No symbolism is shown here and it is almost as though the background is done in such a way as purposely to subdue the minor details in order that the main focal point of the work will be enhanced.

'When I lived before I used to drink blackbirds' blood,' Julie informed her granny, much to the woman's horror. She then went on to say that it tasted sweet.

In some of the drawings there are tiny blackbirds, sometimes seen in flight and sometimes on the ground. The blackbirds are not just standing on the ground as one would expect in a child's drawing, but they are lying down on their backs, or on their sides, as if to indicate that these birds are dead. This probably has some connection with Julie's remarks about drinking blackbirds' blood. The whole idea repels Mrs Tomlinson who says, 'I just can't bear to think about the business of drinking such a thing. Who could imagine anything more ghastly?'

Julie's family never ask her any questions. Says her grandmother, 'It has become a family policy. I think we're all a little bit afraid of what we might hear. There are some things you're better off not knowing.'

Julie was born in Wellingborough, a small town in Northamptonshire, and it is known that many centuries ago there was a strong witch cult in that part of the country. There are records of several witches having been burnt at the stake, but by all accounts this was not the normal method of dealing with them, as they were accepted as a part of life by the community and were more or less allowed to get on with it, unless, as must have been the case in the stake burnings, there had been proven malice to a member of the public. The witches of Wellingborough were allowed to gather in the area which lies behind what is now known as Sheep Street, to the rear of the old Hind Hotel (which is rumoured to be haunted by Oliver Cromwell who once lived there).

One of the most telling of little Julie's drawings shows an odd-looking tree in a field and a witch standing beside a large blazing fire. In the centre of the flames there is a small naked baby. Julie's grandmother just can't understand this at all because normally the little girl loves babies, and like most children of her age she mothers her baby dolls and makes a great fuss of them. 'It doesn't make sense,' says Mrs Tomlinson.

Julie has described how she used to go into the woods at night and light big fires. 'We used to kill sheep,' she says. From what Mrs Tomlinson gathers, the sheep were involved in some kind of sacrifice. 'Julie is absolutely certain that she has lived before as a witch,' says her grandmother, 'and when I hear some of the things she comes out with I'm beginning to think she must indeed have been here before because she certainly never got it from us.'

Girl remembers being in Tay Bridge disaster

Diane Brownlea, *Darlington*

On the evening of 28 December, 1879, as a howling gale ravished the east coast of Scotland, steam engine number 224 pulled out of Burntisland station after picking up the Edinburgh passengers from the ferryboat *William Muir* which had crossed the River Forth to connect with the Dundee train.

Six months earlier the journey from Edinburgh to Dundee would have necessitated two river ferryboat crossings, firstly over the Firth of Forth and then across the River Tay. However, since 1 June the impressive new Tay rail bridge had been open for passenger trains.

The bridge was a stupendous work of engineering, a distance of two miles long and eighty feet above the high water mark of the turbulent Tay. The return fare from Edinburgh to Dundee was seven shillings – equivalent to thirty-five pence.

In one of the carriages on that nightmare journey over a century ago sat a man with four small children – one was a baby boy on his knee, the three other toddlers being two girls and another boy – all huddled round their father on their way to see their grandmother in Dundee.

Inside the compartment the children became restless when the carriage was blasted by the wind and sleet, making it sway heavily from side to side. The roar of the storm frightened the children who one by one started to cry.

In the next compartment a Mr Linton was travelling alone from Edinburgh to St Andrews. Because it was a Sunday the normal rail connection from Leuchars Junction was not scheduled to run, so Mr Linton had arranged for his coach to pick him up at Leuchars to take him on to St Andrews.

When Mr Linton heard the screams of the children in

the next compartment, he was moved to go and offer his assistance to the distraught father, whose wife had stayed behind in Edinburgh with relatives because she was expecting her fifth child.

The young father was trying hopelessly to calm his children who were all four crying pitifully. Mr Linton took one of the little girls on his knee and tried to convince her that everything would be all right but the child could not be comforted.

At Leuchars Junction, the train rattled to a halt and Mr Linton jumped off to check with the station master, Thomas Robertson, that the coach had arrived to take him to St Andrews. 'No, sir,' boomed the station master's voice above the roar of the storm. 'There's no sign of any coach. It's more than likely been held up with the weather.'

Linton then got back on board the train resigning himself to the fact that his coach was not going to arrive. He decided that instead of waiting at the desolate station in such dreadful conditions he would go on to Dundee and take a room at a hotel for the night, then make his way back to St Andrews the following morning by which time he hoped the storm would have subsided.

During this time the stationmaster ordered a check on all the carriage wheels to make sure that everything was in order for the arduous journey over the bridge. It was duly reported to Robertson that the wheel check had been completed, and that he could give the go-ahead for the train to set off on the next lap of the journey which would take them to one more station, St Fort, then on across the bridge and into Dundee.

Before he authorized the departure, Robertson, being a thoughtful conscientious man, braved the elements to take one last look down the winding country road to see if there was any sign of Linton's coach. There, sure enough, in the distance the stationmaster could see the faint glimmer of lights and he recognized that the overdue coach was at last rumbling along towards the station.

He immediately ran to the train to inform Mr Linton

that his coach was about to arrive. Then he helped the man off the train with his baggage and gave the signal for the engine driver to set off towards St Fort and then on to the southern approach to the bridge.

The train slowed down as it passed the signal box on the south bank of the river and signalman Thomas Barclay held out the bridge baton to the fireman on board, a man called John Marshall, who leaned out of his open cab and exchanged a quick greeting with the signalman as he took the baton. Marshall then called over to the engine driver, David Mitchell, to let him know that he had picked up the baton, giving the driver his cue to increase the speed of the engine to the stipulated twenty-five miles an hour which was the maximum speed allowed for passenger trains crossing the bridge.

At precisely 7.14 p.m. Thomas Barclay put through his signal to the box on the northern end of the bridge confirming that the train had safely entered the bridge section. The signalman on duty in the north box was expecting the train to clear his box at 7.19 p.m. The train with seventy-five people on board set out over the Tay Bridge that dark night, never to reach the other side.

The engine driver clung on to his controls in the open cab as he and his fireman tried to shield themselves from the wind and sleet. They braced themselves as the train shuddered on to the most precarious part of the bridge – the part everyone referred to as the 'high girders', so called because at this point the bridge took on the form of a tunnel of iron lattice-work girders over the centre of the River Tay.

As the old engine struggled on, a sudden deafening roar was heard all along the creaking, swaying bridge. Then with one furious blast the supporting columns split apart under the tremendous pressure of the pounding waters. The girders were wrenched loose and the train with all its crew and passengers plunged deep down into the murky waters of the Tay far below.

On the road to St Andrews, as Mr Linton's coach struggled against the howling storm, he could see the curve of the mighty bridge in the distance and he watched the train, nothing more than a moving line of lights, slowly progress across the bridge.

He was watching the line of lights enter the high girders when suddenly from his coach he saw the horrendous sight of the engine with all five carriages and guard's van plough downwards with the heavy girders into the foaming river. He instantly thought of the family of small children as they fell to certain death.

He later described the scene as follows: 'The great gale seemed to gather itself together for one mighty effort and tore down on the bridge with one tremendous thunderous roar and crash.'

Linton stopped his coach and stood horrified as he traced the black line of the bridge to a point where it became nothingness, just a giant space above the waters of the Tay.

A sailor from the training ship *Mars* had been on deck watch on the River Tay fairly near to the bridge at the time and saw the entire incident. He had an excellent view of the train as it moved across the bridge, but as soon as the line of moving lights entered the central girders, the lights suddenly disappeared and there was a long break in the outline of the bridge structure. The sailor heard nothing above the deafening howl of the wind.

Of the seventy-five people who lost their lives in one of the most tragic rail disasters in history, only forty-six bodies were recovered from the river.

More than a hundred years later, a small three-and-a-half-year-old girl from Darlington has strange recurring memories of that winter night so long ago.

Diane Brownlea was playing with a toy case that her grandmother had bought her in Woolworth's. The toddler dressed up two of her dolls and carefully packed her toy case with odds and ends, then announced to her grandmother, 'I'm going to visit my granny in Dundee now.'

Diane's grandmother, Mrs Pemberton, said to her grandchild, 'But I don't live in Dundee, love, I live here in Darlington.' Then thinking for a moment that Diane was referring to her paternal grandmother whom she called Nanny Brownlea, she said, 'You don't mean Nanny Brownlea, do you? She doesn't live anywhere near Dundee. Aren't you thinking of Newcastle?'

Diane then said, 'No, I mean my other granny that I used to go to see in Dundee when I was a little girl before, when I went on the train over the big bridge.'

Mrs Pemberton tried gently to explain to her grandchild that she had never been to Dundee before. She told Diane, 'Dundee isn't even in this country, it's in Scotland. You know you've never been to Scotland, love.'

Diane answered, 'I lived in Scotland when I was here before and my granny lived in Dundee.' Again she insisted that she used to go to visit her granny on the train.

Her grandmother says that she was surprised that Diane could know anything about a bridge and she swears that Dundee had never been mentioned to the child. She explains, 'We have absolutely no connection with Dundee – no relations, no friends, absolutely no one – so no one in the family ever had cause to mention the place. And as far as the granny part goes – well, I'm one of her grannies and Mrs Brownlea, her father's mother, is the other one. She's a Geordie like the rest of her family, with no ties in Scotland at all, and I'm a Darlington woman, born and bred. I've never even been out of England in all my years.'

Then one day about a month later Diane told her, 'I fell into the water when I went to see granny in Dundee.' When her grandmother asked Diane what she meant, she said, 'I was with my other daddy and we all fell into the water when we were on the train.'

From then on Diane constantly repeated that she fell into the water when she was in the train going to see her granny in Dundee. The child of course is too young to know anything about the 1879 disaster. She cannot read and the subject has not been covered on television. In any case Diane is only interested in the children's programmes and that is all she watches.

The child has not mentioned anything about having had brothers or sisters but she does refer to her previous family as 'we all fell into the water'. This would indicate that there were more people involved than just herself and her father who is vivid in her memory. She makes no mention of her mother, only her father.

Apart from Mr Linton who travelled on the doomed train, other people witnessed the family of father and four children on the train on the night of the disaster. At St Fort station, the final stop before the bridge, all the tickets had to be collected from the passengers who were alighting at Dundee, and other travellers going further north through Arbroath, Stonehaven, Aberdeen and even further up the Scottish east coast had their tickets checked.

William Friend, the ticket collector, remarked to the stationmaster after the train pulled out of St Fort station that he had seen a man with three or four small children with him huddled together in one of the compartments. He remembered thinking at the time that the man had a lot on his hands with so many young children on such a foul night. He had collected the man's ticket and noticed that the family were bound for Dundee. He also remarked that there was no sign of the mother in the compartment, and it was this fact that had drawn the collector's attention to the plight of the father.

From this it would seem that there was only the one family of small children on the train that night. The family on the train consisted of a father, two boys (including the baby) and two girls. Could it be that little Diane Brownlea was one of those girls?

Although it is heart-breaking to think of those children going to their watery graves it surely must bring comfort to know that little Diane is a happy, contented, well-adjusted, normal little girl who plays with her dolls and toy case like all little girls love to. If she was one of the girls on that nineteenth-century train then she certainly has come through with flying colours.

Boy remembers being drowned off sailing ship

Simon Brown, *Chelmsford*

Shortly after two-year-old Simon had learnt to hold a conversation, he turned to his mother Susan and surprised her by saying, 'Mummy, I've been here before. I was on a big boat with sails and ropes on it and I fell into the water. I went under the water and died.'

His mother thought that Simon might have been daydreaming, but six months later he repeated the same story, and added that he remembers being in the water, which was very dirty, with his dog who always went everywhere with him.

Simon described the boat as having lots of sails and three masts and hundreds of ropes. He remembers that there had been a fierce storm and he fell overboard. He told his mother that the boat had a giant wheel with spokes all round it and he said that some of the other men used to steer the ship using the wheel. From his reference to other men it would seem that Simon was a grown man in his other life.

Susan says that every now and then Simon comes out with words which she has never heard before, like the time he accidentally knocked over a pot of Susan's freshly-made blackcurrant jam, sending it crashing to the kitchen floor. When he saw how harassed his mother was at having to clean up the sticky mess of jam and broken glass, he looked up at her apprehensively and said, 'I hope I don't have to do haze now, Mummy.' Susan was in no humour for wisecracks and thinking that the child had picked up some slang word she started to tell him off, saying that he must speak properly. Then she asked him what he meant.

Simon answered, 'When I was a sailor I hated doing haze but sometimes I had to.' 'What's haze?' demanded Susan. Her son answered, 'It was what happened when we were naughty. We had to scrub all the decks and do all the work.'

Susan mentioned the incident to Simon's father Greg, after which it was more or less forgotten till one evening an old friend of Simon's father paid a visit to the Brown household. The man, Peter Rawlings, had emigrated to Australia several years previously, and had never seen little Simon as the child had been born since his departure. Peter was an ex-merchant seaman.

After Simon was put to bed the adults settled down to talk about old times. Naturally the conversation got round to ships and the sea. Greg asked Peter if he had ever heard the word haze. Peter replied, 'Of course. Every sailor knows what haze is. It's extra work given on board as punishment.'

Peter explained that in the old days sailors used to dread haze, as it usually meant that they would not only be subjected to incessant hard work, but more often than not they would be refused their quota of rum and often would have to go without regular meals for the period of probation – or haze. As conditions on board were far from ideal even at the best of times, this extra penalty inflicted extreme hardship on a man.

When Simon's parents heard Peter's explanation, they began to take their son's remarks more seriously. They realized that the little boy must have got the unusual word from somewhere, yet they had never heard of the expression before and they were certain that Simon had never been told about haze by anyone. Susan says, 'He knows absolutely no one who could have told him. His father and I can only assume that he really has remembered it from a previous life as a sailor.' Greg is impressed with the way young Simon can describe the ship that he sailed in and some of the places he visited. He says, 'He knows more about a sailing ship than I do. He can tell you all about the different sails and rigging and all that. He's mentioned some things I've never even heard of, like a spanker. He says his boat had a spanker on it – whatever that is.'

Simon must have been a regular crew member although he cannot remember any name or special rank. From the fact that he had been given haze it would appear that he was not an officer.

Susan says, 'He can be playing away as usual and he might look at something, or pick up some object which sets things off in his head and he starts remembering things. The other day he was playing around with an old toy clock. He was staring at it intently and turning it round and round in his hands. He looked up at me and told me that the clock reminded him of the wheel of his ship. He seemed to be in a kind of daze as if he was away in another world.'

Simon remembers being on board the ship for long periods at a time. He must have been on long voyages because he told his mother that when they had been away on the ship, sometimes the men got fed up and would start fighting with each other. He remembers that they were given horrible jobs to do to keep them busy.

Although Simon does not remember any names of places he visited in his sea-faring days, he has vivid pictures in his mind of landing on some kind of island. He says there was lovely sand all round the land and lots of trees, flowers and fruit. They made fires on the shore and they spent some time walking around looking for food, but they slept in their cabins on board.

'The ship was kept near the edge of the water and we had to go back to it every night to sleep,' he says. He remembers eating bananas and other fruits which he could not describe. He told his mother that he has never seen them in the fruit shop.

'It was always hot on the land but we needed to light fires because another sailor told us to.' Simon had no idea why the fires were lit. Perhaps it was to cook their food, or possibly to ward off any wild animals.

When Susan asked her son if he met any people on the land, he replied, 'Lots and lots. They didn't have any clothes on, but they had lots of colours on them and beads.' His mother then asked him if he spoke to the people. He replied, 'They tried to talk to us but we didn't know what they were

92

saying. They talked funny words. They gave us the bananas and other fruit and things.'

Susan asked him if these people looked like him. He told her yes, but they were very sunburnt. From this, Susan is not sure if her little boy meant that the people were coloured, but she gets the impression that they were not. She thinks this, because Simon has a little West Indian friend called Wesley and when she asked Simon if the people looked like Wesley, he said no. She feels that if the natives had been West Indian or Negro then Simon would have said straight away that they were like his little coloured friend.

'I've got a feeling that he may have gone to some of the Polynesian islands,' says Susan. 'Of course that's a long shot as it could be anywhere really.' She comes to the Polynesian conclusion because Simon describes the land as being lush in vegetation, with flowers and fruit in abundance and he says it was very very hot.

Simon told his mother that they played drums and sang funny songs, which according to the boy's description were more of a slow chant. 'The people danced for us and gave us nice things to eat,' he recalls. Susan says, 'This sounds as if they were invited to some kind of feast or celebration. The natives seemed to be very friendly as Simon has no memories of any hostility on the part of the islanders.'

Simon seems to have come to terms with his drowning. Greg explains, 'I would have thought that something as traumatic as being drowned would cause all kinds of havoc in a person's mind – that's assuming that they remember it all as Simon seems to. The peculiar thing is that it doesn't seem to bother him in the slightest. He remembers that his dog was with him throughout the whole ordeal but he doesn't seem to be too put out by the fact that he died. If anything, he makes more fuss about the fact that the water was dirty – as if that makes any difference.'

Greg is somewhat puzzled by Simon's comment about the dirty water. He feels that if the storm had taken place while the ship was out on the open sea then the water would hardly be described as dirty. He wonders if the ship was docked in some big port at the time, because that might explain the dirty water. The argument against that is the obvious one that if the ship was in port during the storm, then there would be no need for the crew to stay aboard. They could easily have gone ashore to safety.

Of course there is always the possibility of Simon having some kind of mishap in these very conditions, i.e. the ship was docked in a big port during a violent storm and while trying to get ashore with his dog, he could have fallen overboard.

Regarding the actual drowning, Simon calmly says, 'It went all black when I went underneath the water. It was very quiet. After a long time I woke up and my dog was with me. We were in a bright place but I was very tired. I went to sleep again.'

He does not remember much about what happened in the interim period but he does remember that he was then re-born and Susan and Greg were his parents. He said to his mother, 'After a long time I came back here and you were my new mummy.'

Susan asked Simon if he was English when he was a sailor. The boy replied, 'I think so. I talked the same as I do now.'

Greg was interested to hear that the odd words used by his young son in connection with his ship are not really so odd to anyone familiar with sailing ships. A spanker, for instance, is a term used to describe the fore-and-aft sail of a ship.

Young Simon is unperturbed about his previous life, and although he knows all about ships he is no more or less enthusiastic about them than anyone else. He takes a very philosophical view and regards his past life as over and done with. He doesn't have any special hankerings for a life at sea. Perhaps he feels that once is enough for anyone.

Small girl remembers being a boy

Sharon Prescott, *Lanark*

Three-and-a-half-year-old Sharon was out shopping with her mother in the small Scottish market town where they live when she said to her mother, 'When I was a boy I lived up round the back of the old church.'

The child's mother Judy looked slightly surprised but just dismissed it as the ramblings of a child with a vivid imagination. A few weeks later Judy was in the same market place and once more little Sharon pointed towards the old church and repeated that when she was a little boy she used to live up the road behind it.

Out of curiosity, Judy said, 'OK. Come on, then. Show me.' With that Sharon took her mother's hand and led her up behind the church, past a children's play park and over a couple of roads. Then Sharon stopped but she seemed to be bewildered, as she stood looking around her.

Judy remembers her reaction at that moment. 'Come on, Sharon,' she said to the child. 'Let's not waste any more time with all this nonsense.'

Although Sharon was looking puzzled she wouldn't move away from the spot. She told her mother, 'But it's all different now, Mummy.' Her mother was quickly losing patience and took hold of her little girl to take her back to the shopping area of town.

Sharon pulled back and said to her mother, 'But I did live here when I was a little boy. I remember it, Mummy, but the houses are all different now.'

That evening Judy told her husband Glen all about the episode with Sharon earlier that day. As the couple talked it over, and Judy described the route that Sharon had led her, it became apparent that they had gone to the area of town where Glen had lived for a short time when he was a small baby.

Judy says, 'I knew that my husband's family had come from that area, but at the time I didn't think anything of it. It was only when Glen and I started to talk things over that we realized that Sharon had stopped at the exact same road where the old family cottage used to stand. You see, I had not known the family when they lived there so I didn't know the district where they used to live.'

Glen and his family had long since lost touch with that area of town and in fact in his early childhood everyone had to be moved out when the entire district came under new development. The old houses were pulled down and all the residents were scattered to various districts of the town and surrounding area.

The whole place was completely gutted and brand new modern homes were built on the site of the old tumble-down cottages. Judy now wonders if this is why Sharon looked so lost when she stood and looked around her at the new different houses. 'She seemed to be completely bewildered because the houses were different,' says Judy. 'But she was adamant that she was in the correct road. She seemed to recognize the route from the main shopping centre of town to where her father used to live without any difficulty whatever. It was just the new buildings that threw her.'

The re-development of the area could well explain why little Sharon was mixed up. Before the new houses the old cottages were home to her great-grandparents for many years. When Glen's father left the family home to get married, he lived for a few years in a neighbouring village with his new wife. He then moved back to the family cottage when Glen was a small baby while they waited for a few months until they got another house of their own. It was only during this short few months that Glen had lived in his grandparent's cottage, but the old couple had lived there for more than thirty years.

Glen wonders if there could be any connection between Sharon and his grandparents, whom the child never met. One day Glen asked Sharon, 'Can you remember what your name was when you were a little girl before?' Sharon answered instantly, 'Oh I wasn't a little girl, Daddy, I was a little boy.' This answer was more than her father had bargained for because he was sure that she had just got mixed up somehow when she had talked before of being a boy, but here again she was quite definite and stated clearly that she was a boy in her previous life. Her father then asked her, 'What are you talking about, Sharon? How could you be a little boy?' His daughter assured him that she had been a boy. Then she added, 'And when I grew up I was a man, and I worked at a big place down the road past Forbes Farm.'

Glen says, 'The Forbes Farm bit shook me because that did exist at one time but it disappeared off the face of the earth years and years ago. It was taken over by the re-developers when all the old cottages were knocked down. It all happened so long ago that nearly everyone's forgotten all about it. Nobody even mentions Forbes Farm any more. I remember hearing my father talking about it.'

He wonders how Sharon would know that there had once been a place called Forbes Farm which was situated in the vicinity of the old cottages. He honestly doesn't feel that anyone could have told the little girl about such a place because she only mixes with the small children of a few of their immediate neighbours – all young couples who came to the district long after Forbes Farm was knocked down.

Glen explains, 'It's not as if the people still call that part by its old name or anything as often happens. When the developers took over they made a clean sweep and re-named all the roads. Forbes Farm was never used as a reference term for any part of the area.'

As for Sharon saying that she worked in a big place down the road past Forbes Farm, Glen can think of two or three possibilities. 'There are a couple of big factories down that way,' he said. 'But the thing that sticks in my mind most is that my old grandfather used to work in a big bakery for a while and that was down past where the old farm road used to be.'

Another link between Sharon and her great-grand-father? Perhaps. The old man used to leave his cottage very early in the mornings to walk down the quiet country road, past the part where the Forbes Farm lane met the road, and down another few hundred yards to the old bakery which also has been long since demolished.

Sharon told Judy that she remembers being a little boy very well. She says, 'I had a lovely cat called Nutty.' She remembers how Nutty used to scamper around the cottage looking for mice. She used to run after Nutty and help him find the mice for her mother.

Sharon says, 'My other mummy cried when I was a little boy.' When Judy asked her what had happened to make her mother cry, Sharon answered, 'It was a bad woman that made her cry.' The child would not say anything further at that point. Judy could see that her little daughter was becoming quite upset. She says, 'Sharon went very quiet and her face became deadly serious. She had tears in her eyes as if she was remembering something which had upset her deeply at some time.'

Several weeks after, while Glen was pushing Sharon on her garden swing, she suddenly shouted to her father, 'Stop. Stop, Daddy, I want to get off!' Glen says, 'She sounded so frightened I stopped the swing instantly. I couldn't understand it because she always loves to be pushed on her swing, and usually I'm the one that gets fed up with it before she does.'

From Sharon's swing, she could see out beyond the back garden of their home on to the roadway. She had spotted something which seemed to terrify her. As soon as she got off her swing she grabbed her father's hand and pulled at him to go into the house.

She kept crying, 'Bad woman's coming – bad woman's coming.' Glen looked out towards the roadway but could see no one. Because Sharon was getting herself worked up into such a state he took the child into the house and tried to calm her down. He assured the little girl that there was no bad woman anywhere. Sharon shouted in a frightened tone, 'I saw her, Daddy. She's coming to get us. She's the bad woman.'

The next moment someone knocked on the side door of the house. At this, little Sharon started screaming uncontrollably as she ran to Judy. She kept repeating to her parents, 'Don't answer. Don't go to the door.'

Glen answered the door to find a middle-aged gypsy woman standing there trying to sell him some trinkets out of a small case and offering to read his fortune. Glen looked at the woman suspiciously. He had never seen her in the area before but he felt compelled to ask her if she had been down their road before. The woman told him that she had not and that it was all new territory to her.

She was an Irish gypsy, well graced with the gift of the gab, and promised Glen every good fortune under the sun, providing he would cross her palm with silver, just, as she put it, 'to help keep an oul' woman's body and soul together'.

Glen told the woman that he wanted no fortune read and he warned her not to come back near the house ever again, and he told her to tell her friends to stay away as well.

When he went back inside he found his little daughter crying her eyes out. He told her that everything was fine and that she had nothing to worry about. Sharon sobbed, 'That's the bad woman that made my other mummy cry.' The story came out that when Sharon was a little boy, a gypsy woman had knocked at the door of their cottage and when her mother answered it the woman said that she was a fortune teller. Sharon remembers the woman asking for her hand to be crossed with silver, but as soon as the gypsy saw that there was no sale for her fortune-telling she screamed abuse and said that she was going to cast an evil spell on the family.

This had upset and frightened Sharon's other mother so much that the woman had burst into tears. The memory of that event was so strongly stamped on the child's mind that as soon as she saw the gypsy walking up the road towards their house something sparked in the little girl's head and rekindled the memory of what had happened with the gypsy and her mother in her previous life.

Glen explains, 'We hardly ever get peddlars or gypsy fortune-tellers around here, but seemingly years ago they were quite common. There was a camp of Irish gypsies on some waste ground not far from the old cottages. They were harmless enough but they became a nuisance, always trying to flog things. The fortune-telling was quite a novelty at first, but the people soon got tired of it. There were too many gypsies and they were constantly knocking on doors begging for money. The people in the cottages hardly had any money themselves. These gypsy women had fierce tempers and they had a nasty habit of casting what they reckoned were evil spells if they didn't get what they wanted.'

Glen continues, 'Of course it was all a lot of old bunk, but the old biddies could be so convincing with their threats that it would have been very unpleasant to be on the receiving end of their wrath.'

There is no question that Sharon recognized the same woman, but there must have been something familiar about the gypsy who walked up their back garden path and knocked on the side door of their house that day.

Judy says, 'Most of those women look the same anyway. They all have red cheeks and high cheekbones and they usually wear their hair tied back behind their ears, and they nearly all wear scarves over their heads. Because they spend so much time out of doors their complexions are ruddy and rather coarse-looking. They are usually on the hefty side.'

It is not so surprising, then, that as Sharon spied the gypsy woman from her swing her memory immediately raced back to the time that she had seen a woman who looked very similar say upsetting things to her previous mother.

Little Sharon's parents have since explained to her that although the woman who frightened her other mummy was not a very nice sort of person that doesn't mean that all gypsy women are the same. They told her gypsies are just like everyone else: some of them are nice and some are a bit silly.

'I think she understands,' says Judy. 'She's fine now, but she still talks about how that bad woman made her other mummy cry. I don't think she'll ever forget that.'

Glen has a feeling that there is some kind of bond between his grandfather and his daughter. 'I can't say definitely what it is,' he says, 'but so many things seem to click together.'

There is always the possibility, of course, that the link could be with some other member of the family who lived in the little cottage at some period in their lives. The mystery remains unsolved, but it doesn't seem to bother little Sharon, whose fondest memories seem to centre round Nutty her cat.

Boy remembers being a commando

Stephen Ramsay, *Blackpool*

From the time that Stephen was only twelve months old he has had a terrible fear of planes. Any time a plane would pass over his home he would become hysterical. At first, his mother Tessa thought that it was just the noise that was upsetting her baby and that he would eventually grow out of it.

Very early one morning, before the alarm clock went off, Stephen, who was then two years old, scrambled out of his little bed and ran into his parents' room, climbed into the bed beside his mother and shook her to wake her up, calling out, 'There's a plane coming, Mummy. There's a plane coming.' His mother could hear nothing and she told the child that he must have been dreaming. Stephen then said, 'I don't like planes because a plane hurt my tummy once.'

Stephen's mother listened carefully, and again she could hear nothing, so she said, 'No, love, there's no plane and anyway you are safe with me.' Within one minute a jet screamed overhead. Tessa hugged Stephen tightly as she wondered how on earth he could have known that a plane was coming. She says, 'He seemed to be able to sense that the plane was on its way. I can't believe that he could have heard anything because it was so early in the morning and there wasn't a sound. I'm sure I would have heard it if he heard it.'

Tessa remembers feeling very odd one sunny afternoon when they had just finished lunch. Her husband Bill, Stephen and herself were just about to get up from the table when a jet screamed over the house. Stephen instantly dropped onto his stomach and crawled commando-style under the table. Tessa remembers, 'He did it with such speed and in such a professional way that it really made my hair bristle, although I know that sounds silly.' After the noise of the jet died away Stephen, still lying flat out under the table, called out, 'OK. It's all clear now.' Then the little boy crawled out from under the table.

About a year after that incident, when Stephen was three, Bill was playing around the house with him when the child started to rub his stomach and said to his father, 'I got my tummy hurt with a plane once, Daddy.' Bill just laughed and picked his little boy up, thinking that this was just another example of the child showing his fear of planes. 'Oh, you don't want to worry about planes,' said his father. 'You'll see when you get older; they just look big and they sound very loud but they won't come near you or hurt you.'

'A plane hurt me in my tummy,' repeated Stephen. Bill tried to talk things through with his little son to explain to him that he was only imagining that he had hurt his tummy because he was afraid of planes. Bill said, 'So you see a plane didn't really hurt your tummy, you just think it did.' Stephen started to nod his little head frantically saying, 'It did, Daddy, it did. The plane did hurt my tummy.' Bill looked at his child seriously and was just about to make another attempt to reason with Stephen, when the little boy said, 'It was when I lived the last time, before I died.'

Bill was taken aback at Stephen's words and repeated aghast, 'Before you died?' Stephen went on to say, 'I died when that plane hurt my tummy.' By now Bill was beginning to think that there might be something in what Stephen was saying. He recalls, 'It was the way that he came right out with it without any hesitation that made me think twice. When he said that he had died I got a bit of a shock because that's not the kind of thing he would be likely to say. In fact he had never said anything like that before – about having died – although he had always been absolutely terrified of planes.'

Stephen then told his father, 'I was a big man then and we had to hide from the planes.' Bill remembered how

Stephen had crawled under the table the time that he heard the jet and he wondered if there could be a connection. The two incidents seemed to match up.

'Why did you hide from the planes?' asked his father. The child answered, 'Because the planes were trying to hurt us.' His father asked Stephen, 'But why should they want to hurt you?' Stephen explained, 'Because we were all fighting in the trees.' Bill asked him, 'Where were these trees?' Stephen told him, 'I don't know, but there were lots of trees and it was hot all the time.'

With a question here and there, Bill learnt from Stephen that he had been fighting in a very hot place which sounded as if it could be a jungle and that Stephen was with a crowd of other men. They were being attacked from the air by low-flying planes, but there was also some fighting on the ground. The planes would sweep down towards Stephen and his men and drop bombs.

The little boy remembers, 'The planes made loud bangs and they tried to kill us.' He told his father, 'We tried to hide in the trees when we heard the planes coming but one time a plane came down and hurt my tummy.' 'What happened then?' asked Bill. Stephen replied, 'That was when I died. My tummy got hurt and it was bleeding.' Bill asked Stephen if he knew what happened then and the little boy replied, 'I just went to sleep in the trees.' Bill asked him, 'Do you remember what happened then?' Stephen replied, 'After I was sleeping I woke up and my tummy was all better.' Bill asked him where he was then and his son said, 'I was still in the trees.' When asked what happened after that Stephen told his father, 'A lady came to see me.'

'What lady?' asked Bill. The child replied, 'She was a nice lady and she told me to follow her. She took my hand and took me with her.' Bill asked what happened next and Stephen replied, 'She took me to a nice place and told me to go back to sleep again.' When asked where the place was, Stephen replied, 'It was where lots of beds and seats were.'

Bill thought for a moment that his child was trying to describe some kind of hospital. He said, 'Was it a hospital with sick people in it, Stephen?' His son replied, 'No. The people weren't sick, they were just tired.' Bill asked his son if he remembered anything about after that and Stephen said, 'I wakened up sometimes and went back to sleep again.'

'Did you see anyone in this place?' asked Bill. Stephen said, 'Oh yes, the nice lady was with me all the time.' When Bill asked if he knew the lady's name or anything about her, Stephen said thoughtfully, 'I don't know her name, but she told me that I had to sleep because I had died.' Then he added, 'She said I had to get strong again.'

When asked what the lady looked like, Stephen said, 'She had a blue dress on.' 'Was it an ordinary dress?' asked Bill, 'or was it long?' After a few moments of thinking, Stephen said, 'It wasn't too long and it wasn't too short.' Bill asked Stephen if the lady's dress was like his mummy's dresses and the boy replied, 'Kind of like them.'

'Do you remember what happened after that?' asked Bill, and Stephen told him, 'I had to wait around for a long time.' His father asked him, 'Well, what were you waiting for?' and the little boy replied, 'Till it was time for me to come to you and Mummy.'

'Really?' exclaimed Bill, not knowing quite what to think. Then he asked Stephen, 'Well, how did you know when it was time for you to be born again?' Stephen said, 'Oh, they always come and tell you when you're going to be born.' 'Who's they?' asked Bill. His son told him, 'They're the men who looked after all the people.' Bill said, 'So there were lots of other people in this place?' and Stephen replied, 'Oh yes, Daddy. I had lots and lots of friends there.' 'Well, what did you and your friends do?' asked Bill. 'Did you work or play or what?' 'Oh we had work to do if we wanted to do it,' said Stephen. Then he added, 'But we didn't have to do it.' His father asked him, 'Well, what work did you do then?' Stephen's answer left

Bill really puzzled. The child told his father, 'I worked in the library.'

Bill didn't think that Stephen really knew what a library was, but he thought perhaps the child had heard his mother talk about their local library because both he and his wife were members. Bill said, 'Are you thinking about Mummy's and Daddy's library, Stephen?' The child replied, 'No, my library was much bigger than yours. It was a giant library.'

Still wary, Bill said, 'Well what did you do in the library, Stephen?' Again the child's answer left his father very bewildered. Stephen said, 'I had to put all the new bits into the books.' Bill asked, 'What do you mean by the new bits?' The child answered, 'Sometimes the books were wrong and I had to make them right for people.'

'For what people?' asked Bill. Stephen answered, 'For the people who wrote the books, of course.' Bill asked Stephen if he knew the names of these people and the child hesitantly replied, 'I can't remember. I don't know. I didn't talk to them much.' Bill asked him how he knew what to change in the books and the child replied, 'I got to know.' Bill asked him if the people who wrote the books told him what new bits he had to put into them and Stephen answered, 'Not them, the other people told me. The ones who looked after us all.'

Stephen went on to explain to his father that there were lots of people living together but over these people there resided a few other men in charge of them. When Bill asked him if he meant that the people in charge were like kings, Stephen said that they didn't call the men kings. He told his father that the men who instructed him on what he had to add into the library books were the same men that informed him about when he was to be born again. He said that he thinks he called the men by their names but he couldn't remember what the names were.

When the child started play-school at the age of four, most of his memories were pushed to the back of his mind, although it took him quite a while to get over his fear of planes.

Tessa says, 'It's funny because although Stephen was terrified of planes right up until recently when he started school, he seemed just to have the feeling of fear without knowing why. Yet when he was much younger he would say that he was afraid because a plane hurt his tummy. He never seemed to associate the planes he heard later on with the business about being killed by a plane in his previous life.' Then Tessa adds, 'I suppose now that he's coming to terms with the fear of planes, I wouldn't be surprised if eventually he forgets that he was ever even afraid at all. He seems to be so taken up with school and all the new things that he's learning that he doesn't have much room for anything else in his head.'

Girl remembers Jesus

Lorna Taylor, *Plymouth*

From the time she was an eighteen-month-old baby, little Lorna has been able to hear and see people outside the range of normal perception. She used to laugh and giggle in her cot, and wave her arms in the air as if she was reaching for some toy which was being dangled in front of her then taken away suddenly, making the child miss catching the invisible object each time. This game would never fail to send the baby into hoots of happy laughter, but the strange thing was that Lorna's mother Margaret could never see anyone else in the baby's room.

Margaret says, 'It was just as if someone was waving a toy in front of her then pulling it back suddenly just before she could grab it. She would throw out her arms quickly and stretch out her little fingers just as if she was trying to catch something.' Margaret says that she could see by studying her baby's face that the child was definitely focusing on someone. 'Her gaze was fixed on an area just above her cot as if someone was standing there playing with her. Sometimes her eyes would move slightly but she seemed to be holding someone in focus all the time. It was as if the person would move slightly and Lorna's eyes would follow. I often wondered who my baby's mystery playmate was. I imagine whoever it was must have been an adult because of the way Lorna would look upwards above the top rail of her cot at much the same angle as she would look up at me. One thing's for sure, she was very much at home with her playmate, as she had such a happy contented expression on her face every time I would find her playing her little game.'

Margaret says that she can't remember a time when Lorna didn't understand what was being said to her. 'She has always been completely aware of what was going on around her, and whatever I said to her I got the impression that she understood my message. Something in her eyes and her knowing expression would tell me that she was following my words and that she knew what they meant.'

When Lorna was two years old Margaret's father died. Even at that young age, Lorna seemed to have an inner knowledge of death and birth and she seemed to accept these things as being perfectly natural and nothing to get alarmed about. Margaret said that Lorna came up to her, put her arms around her mother's neck and said, 'I know you're sad, Mummy, but Grandad's with Jesus and his mummy and daddy now and all his pain has gone.'

A few days after, Lorna said to her mother, 'I expect when I'm old I'll be quite glad to die, because everybody I love will be with Jesus and I'll want to be there too.' Margaret asked Lorna what made her think that, and the child replied, 'Because I used to be with Jesus before I was born.' Margaret asked Lorna how she knew that it was Jesus and the child replied, 'Everybody knew it was Jesus when He came to see us. Everybody talked about Him coming.' Margaret then asked Lorna where she was when she saw Jesus and Lorna answered, 'It was when I was at my other home before I was born.'

Margaret persevered, asking her daughter, 'But where was this other home?' Lorna replied, 'It's where everyone lives before they're born.' 'I don't remember being there,' said Margaret. Her daughter told her, 'Of course you were there and so was Daddy but you're too old to remember.' In spite of herself Margaret had to laugh. She then went on to tell Lorna that she has never remembered being in a place with Jesus, even when she was a little girl. Lorna's answer staggered Margaret. The child told her mother, 'Of course you remembered when you were a baby, but you've forgotten it all now you're old.'

Lorna's father David was bemused when Margaret told him what their little girl had been saying. He thought that he would try to find out what was putting those thoughts into the child's mind. She had been taken to Sunday school a couple of times and he thought that perhaps something had been said which Lorna had possibly misinterpreted.

David asked Lorna, 'Remember that time when you went to Sunday school, love? Was that when you heard all this about Jesus?' Lorna replied instantly, 'No. I didn't see Jesus at Sunday school, only Mr Edwards.' (Mr Edwards is the local vicar.) Lorna's father was quite glad that his small daughter recognized the difference.

David then asked Lorna, 'But did you see any pictures of Jesus, and did that make you think you'd seen him?' Lorna answered, 'Oh I did see pictures of Him in my book, but I liked Him better when I saw Him really.' Again David pressed on to try to get to the bottom of the question. He said, 'But didn't you just imagine you saw Him? Like when you have a dream?' Lorna was emphatic in her reply. 'No, Daddy, I didn't dream about Jesus. He came to see us when I lived at my other home.'

'What other home?' asked her father. She replied sharply, 'The home I lived in before I was born.' Lorna was getting slightly peeved at having to repeat herself so many times, so her father thought that he would let things rest for a while.

When the child started play-school her teacher told Margaret that she was very much ahead of the other children and that she didn't really act like a child at all. She never had to be disciplined and she seemed to know instantly what to do with everything. Her teacher particularly noticed that Lorna was very considerate of the other children's feelings, and says, 'She is acutely aware of when anyone is upset. Sometimes when I get a bit harassed if the children get boisterous or have tiffs with one another, I notice that Lorna looks at me in such an understanding way as if she really appreciates how I must be feeling. She has such a lovely comforting face that I always feel better. I feel as if she is more of a little friend than a child.'

Margaret says that since Lorna started play-school it is almost as if she is slowly learning to become a child.

However she constantly says things that reveal a mind which is far from child-like.

Once Margaret and Lorna were in the centre of Town waiting in the parked car for David to join them. Margaret recalls how they were just sitting quietly, looking out of the windows when all at once Lorna turned to her mother and said, 'I know where all these people came from.' Then she went on to say, 'There was a time once when there were no people, no cars or houses, just trees and grass and sky. I wonder where the first lady and man came from to make all these people?' Lorna had just turned three when she said this.

Lorna seems to have a deep understanding about personal relationships and she can analyse these. When she started play-school she met lots of other children for the first time. She told her mother, 'As soon as I saw Georgina I knew I liked her, and although I was shy at first, the more I knew her the more I liked her. That's what being friends is, isn't it?' Margaret told Lorna that she was glad that she had a nice new friend at play-school. Then Lorna said, 'I thought Noreen was a friend but she just stands in the doorway, and the first person who comes up, she says hello to, and that's her friend for the playtime.' Then Lorna added, 'That's not a real friend, is it, Mummy?'

When Lorna was three-and-a-half she was sitting with her father, and she suddenly said, 'Jesus wasn't with us all the time, you know, Daddy.' 'Oh really?' answered her father. She went on, 'No. He only came to see us on special days and we all went out to see Him.'

Again David thought that he would try to find out just what was making her say such things. Now she had started play-school he realized that there were more people influencing her life, and her levels of knowledge were rising all the time. He wondered if someone had said anything to start her talking about Jesus again.

He asked her, 'Have you been getting stories about Jesus at play-school, love?' She answered, 'We were practising for our Christmas play about Jesus, and Mrs

Dodds (her play-school teacher) said that when we die and go to Heaven, Jesus is with us all the time.' Then she added in a confident tone, 'He's not, you know – not all the time. We can't see Him all the time but I think He can see us.'

'How do you know He's not?' asked her father. 'Because I remember. He only used to come to see us sometimes,' came the reply. David argued, 'But you haven't died yet, Lorna, so how could you know?' She replied, 'I died the last time, but when I went to my other home I didn't see Jesus all the time.' Then she added most adamantly, 'Not all the time.'

'What do you mean by when you died the last time?' David asked her. She replied, 'The last time I died when I was here before.' He argued, 'But you've never been here before, love.' She looked him straight in the eye and said slowly, 'Oh yes I have, but you weren't my daddy then.'

David just looked at his little daughter, not quite knowing what to say next. He remembers feeling a funny sensation flow over him as she said the words. He recalls, 'There was just something in the slow deliberate way she said it that made my blood creep. It was as if she was letting me in on some deep mysterious secret. I wasn't sure that I wanted to hear any more right at that moment.'

After he pulled himself together, Lorna's father said to her, 'Oh really? Well, who was your daddy?' She looked very thoughtful and then she said, 'I don't know, but I know I had another mummy as well.' David asked her, 'How do you know that, then?' She replied, 'I know I had because I had a daddy and a mummy.' David continued, 'O.K., who was your mummy then?' Again the child hesitated, then said, 'I don't know who she was but I know I had one.' Her father asked her, 'What happened to them?' She answered, 'I don't know. When I was little I got sick and then that was when I died and went back to Jesus.' Then as an afterthought she added quite categorically, 'But He wasn't with us all the time, Daddy.'

By that time David had got the message. In the after-life which Lorna had often talked about, Jesus only came to visit her and her friends sometimes, not all of the time.

He said, 'O.K., O.K. So He only came to see you sometimes. What was He like when He did visit you?' Lorna replied, 'He didn't visit me to come to my house like Aunty Jane visits me. He just came to see us.'

'O.K.,' said David, smiling at this. 'When He came to see you, what was He like?' Little Lorna's face lit up into a delightful smile. She told her father, 'He was laughy.'

David roared with laughter when he heard this. He explains, 'The last thing I expected her to say was that.' He put the question to his small daughter another way and asked her, 'What else was He like?' She replied, 'He was pretty and had shiny eyes and He made us all glad, and He had some other people with Him.' When David asked Lorna who the other people were, she told her father that she didn't know their names but that they were Jesus's friends.

David asked Lorna if Jesus said anything. She replied, 'He doesn't talk the same way as we do here. He did talk in a different way but not with saying words.' David asked her what Jesus had said and she hesitated, then replied, 'He came to bring us some light, I think.' Then she repeated slowly, 'He came with bright light to help us.'

David got a feeling that his little daughter was remembering something of profound supernatural value. He remembers, 'She seemed to be awestruck and her face had the most unusual expression on it. She had been smiling a moment earlier when she mentioned about Jesus being laughy but now she had a strange mystified look on her face.'

As Lorna grew older, the memories of Jesus and her life in her other home seemed gradually to vanish, although she is still very much aware of everything around her.

She is now a lively five-year-old and has just started infants' school which she loves. She has two smaller brothers who, as Margaret puts it, are 'much loved and very normal little boys who came into the world with puckered faces, and although very special to my husband and me they are in no way extraordinary.' Recently, Lorna's two-year-old brother Duncan was quite naughty. Margaret told him off and the little boy began to cry, saying that his mummy didn't love him any more. Lorna took her brother's hand in a comforting way and in a worldly voice told him, 'Yes she does love you. She always loves you, she just doesn't like you very much at the moment.' Despite Margaret feeling cross, she was forced to laugh at the way her five-year-old had summed things up absolutely correctly. She says, 'Lorna just seems to know the score. It makes me wonder where she got all this inner knowledge from, as she couldn't have learnt everything since she came to us.'

Girl remembers being a musician

Charlotte Middleton-Million, *Leeds*

Ever since tiny Charlotte could stand up she has had a most amazing sense of rhythm, and when looking through her mother's mail-order catalogues she always used to go straight to the guitar sections and sit and stare at them and try to finger the instruments.

Although Charlotte still hasn't reached her second birthday, so many unaccountable incidents have taken place that her mother Alyson is certain that her baby must have been here before.

'I feel that in Charlotte's past life she must have been involved with music,' says Alyson, 'because apart from her fascination with guitars, a strange thing happened which made me feel more sure than ever that this must be so.'

Alyson says, 'When Charlotte was eighteen months old, I was doing the housework one day and she was playing about with her dolls. The radio was on and a particular record was being played, which featured a prominent piano. Charlotte immediately threw her dolls down and sat upright, her arms out in the air, and started to mime to the music. She moved her fingers separately as if she actually was playing the piano. I was tickled at this, and also surprised because she has never even seen a piano let alone played one – not even a toy one.'

Jokingly, Charlotte's mother asked her, 'Who do you think you are – Chopin?' 'She became very excited, her face became flushed and she started nodding her head furiously as if she was trying to tell me that I was nearly correct. Then she blurted out in her baby voice, "Me playing, me playing." And then she went on miming to the piano music.'

Alyson says that her baby was trying so hard to tell her something, but the child did not know the correct words to use to express herself. 'It was as if she was in agony trying so desperately to communicate with me,' says her mother.

When the child heard the name Chopin she seemed to recognize it even though the name had never been mentioned in her presence before.

'Her reaction really was incredible,' says Alyson. 'I feel deeply that I was on the right track when I said the word Chopin to her, because I saw her eyes instantly light up and her expression was strange as if she was trying to encourage me to keep guessing so I would have eventually hit upon the right name.'

Charlotte's mother feels that it would be all too easy to say that Charlotte had been Chopin in a previous life. She does not believe this, as she explains. 'I'm certain that the name Chopin is only a clue, not the answer. There was something in the way that Charlotte was trying to guide my thoughts, as if her eyes were willing me to keep talking just a little longer and I would have discovered her former identity.' Alyson wonders what would have happened if she had tried another few names.

Other incidents also make Alyson think that her baby has lived before, like the many times the child picks up a baby vest, but instead of putting it on herself or on her dolls as one might expect a child of her age to do, she bundles the vest up and very efficiently goes round all the furniture dusting it. Most people would say that Charlotte must have seen her mother dust the furniture but Alyson thinks that there is more to it than that. 'If the dusting was just an isolated incident then it would not mean much, but when this is seen in an all-over context and all the other things are taken into consideration, it takes on a certain significance,' says Alyson.

Another time they went visiting to Alyson's parents' home, which has a large fireplace in the lounge. Although the chimney has been boarded up for several years, the mantelpiece, grate and hearth are still the main centre feature in the room. Charlotte picked up a small orna-mental brass shovel and began to push this back and forward under the grate as one would do when trying to clean out the ashes of a coal fire. Alyson says that Charlotte could not possibly have copied those actions from anyone because they know absolutely nobody with a coal fire.

Although the child is still very young in earthly terms, Charlotte's mother gets the impression that her little girl is really a very mature person in a baby shell. She says, 'A few days after Charlotte was born I was being visited by my parents who were seated one at each side of the bed. Charlotte was facing my mother when my father made a comment about Charlotte, and the baby turned her head and looked him directly in the eyes. Charlotte has always supported her own head and she has been able to focus properly from day one.'

When her mother first let Charlotte see money, the child seemed to know instinctively what it was for, and when she is given a pen and paper she doesn't scribble as most tiny children of her age would do. She makes a lot of carefully written marks that look like shorthand, all set out in neat rows.

Charlotte is meticulously tidy and clean and has a fantastic sense of humour. Since the age of three months she has had an infectious cheeky laugh, and when she wakes up in the mornings she has a look in her eyes that tells her mother that she is truly glad to be alive. One evening her mother heard giggles coming from her cot and when she went to find out what was so funny Charlotte said, 'Pretty lady makes Charlotte laugh.' Alyson could see no lady.

Her mother says, 'Each day she seems so eager to show me how much she already knows.' The little girl's latest achievement is to stand on a table with her hands on her hips doing a clog dance.

'There are so many things that she does,' says Alyson, 'that I can't believe she has just picked them up in the short time she has been with us. Some of her actions are so automatic that it makes me feel that she has an inbuilt knowledge of what things are all about.'

Boy remembers being his own grandfather

Richard Williamson, *Wootton Bassett*

Richard's parents were discussing an event which had taken place several years before he was born. The two-and-a-half-year-old boy was tinkering away on the floor with his toy cars and seemed to be fully absorbed in what he was doing, so much so that his parents almost forgot that he was in the room.

They had been talking about Richard's grandfather who had died nine months before Richard was born, and they were recalling the time when the old man had suffered a minor accident and had cut his hand when a chisel he had been working with had slipped under the weight of a hammer. Richard's grandfather had to go to the local hospital casualty department where he had four stitches put in his hand.

The boy looked up from his toy cars and said, 'My hand was sore that time.' His mother Frances corrected him and said, 'You mean your grandad's hand was sore.' Richard replied, 'No, my hand, Mummy.' Then he stretched out his left hand and pointed to a spot between his thumb and forefinger and said, 'It was just there, and it was sore, but it's all better now.'

There was no mark or scar of any description on the child's hand but he had pointed to the exact spot which corresponded with the injury received by his grandfather.

Frances had never discussed her father's accident before and she couldn't understand how Richard could have known the location of the injury. She says, 'It wasn't as if my dad's accident had been a major catastrophe or anything like that, so there was never any real reason to mention it. It was just something that had happened to him during his lifetime. The only reason I had been talking about it was that a friend of my husband had hurt his hand the day before and had to have it stitched and that reminded me about my father's similar experience.'

When Richard's father Len asked him how he knew which hand his grandfather had to have the stitches in, the little boy replied, 'I know because it was my hand. I remember.' 'How could you remember?' asked his father. 'You weren't even born when it happened.' The child replied, 'But I was born, Daddy, when I was living before.'

Frances and Len looked at each other and burst into laughter. They tried in vain to explain to their young son that it was impossible for him to remember his grandfather's accident, but no amount of talking could alter Richard's opinion. He assured them that he was the one who had hurt his left hand with the hammer and the 'other big thing' when he was here before.

A few months after this incident the family moved from Surrey to Northampton, which was an entirely new area and one to which little Richard had never been before in his life. Two days after they had arrived at their new home, Richard asked his mother, 'Can we go to York Road today, Mummy?' His mother asked him, 'Where on earth is York Road?' She was still finding her bearings in the new town. Richard replied, 'You know, York Road where I went to when I was living before.' Frances told him, 'You've never been to such a place.' Then, determined to put an end to Richard's stories about having been here before, she took her son out to show him that it was all just a figment of his imagination.

They went down the road and Frances asked the first person they met for directions to York Road, expecting to be told that the person had never heard of such a place. To her amazement the stranger started giving her clear directions of how to get to the place that Frances was sure didn't exist.

When they left the stranger, little Richard turned to his mother and said, 'Why did you ask that man, Mummy? I know how to get there.' By this time Frances was so bewildered that she just let Richard lead her along the road to see what would happen. The child did not follow the instructions his mother had been given, however, so fearing that they might get lost in the new town, Frances remarked to Richard that she thought he might be taking the wrong route. The directions dictated that they should turn right at a certain set of traffic lights. Richard had turned left instead.

'It's O.K., Mummy,' said Richard confidently. 'This is my short-cut.' A few minutes later, to the astonishment of Frances, there they stood looking up at the road sign: York Road.

'Well, where do you want to go to in York Road?' asked Frances. Her son told her that he wanted to see the old shop again where he used to buy his cigarettes. 'We wandered up and down the road several times,' says Frances, but Richard never found his shop. He hesitated at two or three spots but then he seemed to rule them out for some reason, saying that they weren't the same.

Years before Frances's father got married he used to live and work in Northampton. Frances feels that there must be some link between her son, her father, and York Road, although she cannot recall her father having any connections with that particular area. 'At least he never mentioned the place to me,' she says. 'But of course he could easily have known the area in his younger days when he lived in the town. He was a builder and was sent all over the place on various jobs, so this could explain it. Some of the York Road area of Northampton has been changed throughout the years, so that could explain why Richard didn't recognize his shop.'

Richard told his mother that he knew a big red pub that he used to go to when he was living before and it was somewhere on a hill going up towards a park, and it was two roads away from where he used to live. Frances is not entirely sure of the location of the pub on the hill that Richard referred to. She is under the impression that when her little boy mentioned this he was not thinking of York Road but of a different area of Northampton.

When Richard was tiny, he was very attached to his home, and he would get most upset if his parents took him away for the weekend or on a day visit anywhere. As his mother says, 'He would be miserable, unsettled, and a thorough nuisance.'

However, when he was taken to visit Frances's step-mother, he was perfectly happy and contented and as good as gold. Most children love visiting their grand-parents but Frances's step-mother was not Richard's grandmother.

Frances says, 'Although Richard does not look like my father he has the same mannerisms and personality. It sounds a bit silly, but I really feel that my father's spirit lives in Richard. My father died in January and Richard was born the following February. He has the same way of expressing himself and he likes the things that my father used to like.'

Richard is continually making statements about when he used to live before, and many of them correspond with events which took place in the life of his grandfather. Len, his father, says, 'He is always so definite about the things that he remembers. It's not as if he has hazy recollections about things, he seems to remember everything so distinctly.'

Len is entirely and utterly convinced that his little boy has lived before. 'I'd stake my life on it,' he says. 'There's a lot of things that might seem strange to us but that doesn't mean that they don't happen. I personally believe that we do come back again for any number of reasons, although I can't pretend to know the ins and outs of it. After listening to Richard I feel sure it happens.'

Richard informed his parents, 'I'm not frightened of dying because it happened to me before. It was O.K.'

His mother says, 'Whenever he recalls an incident or if he relates a story to us, he always phrases it in the same way. He will say this or that thing happened to him when he was living before; not when he was alive before or when he was here before, but quite definitely when he was living before. It's beyond me. I just can't make head or tail of it. I've heard of odd things like this before but I never thought it could happen in my own family.'

Boy remembers being a ghost

Alexander Dennison, *Rochester*

A few months after Alexander's second birthday his family moved to Kilburn in London. Because the flat was in such a terrible state and badly needed cleaning, Alexander's aunt Brenda said that she would put the child in his pushchair and take him out for a walk so that Irene his mother could have some peace to get on with the cleaning.

Irene explains, 'I had not long started when Brenda came rushing back into the flat looking as white as a sheet. She told me that she would never take Alexander out again as he had nearly frightened the life out of her.' When Irene asked her sister what she meant, Brenda told her that she had walked down Willesden Lane by the old graveyard when Alexander had suddenly pointed towards the gravestones and said, 'Look, roses. That's where I was sleeping when I was a real big man.' Brenda got such a fright that she felt the hair on the nape of her neck stand on end.

Brenda then asked Irene if she had ever taken the baby down that road before. Irene explains, 'I didn't even know where she was talking about. We had only just moved into the flat that morning and although I had gone to view it once before, I had just gone straight to the flat and away again. I didn't know anything about the surrounding roads at all.' Irene goes on to say that even on that one occasion when she had gone to Kilburn to view the flat, she hadn't taken Alexander with her. She had left the child with Brenda while she went to Kilburn herself. Irene adds, 'We didn't even have a television so Alexander couldn't have seen any graveyards on any programme and it's definitely not the kind of thing I would ever talk to a two-year-old about.'

Although Irene was puzzled she thought it best to forget the whole incident and so she put it to the back of her mind. However, six months later, Alexander was sitting in the flat having his dinner when he suddenly said to his mother, 'Mummy, you know when I was a real big man, I died.' The same uncomfortable feeling that Irene had experienced when Brenda told her about the graveyard incident swept over her. 'Did you really?' she replied, trying to sound matter-of-fact. He replied, 'Yes. It was when I was lying under the ground that time.' Irene's heart skipped a beat when she heard this. 'What do you mean, darling?' she asked him. He told her that he remembered lying under the ground, and that there were roses on top of the grass.

Irene was starting to get quite frightened by this time but she noticed that her son didn't seem to be the least bit upset. She asked Alexander, 'How did it feel when you were under the ground?' The child chirped up, 'Oh I wasn't bothered because I wasn't hurting any more.' Irene asked him, 'What had been hurting you?' Alexander replied, 'When I was hurt in the war my tummy and legs were all sore, but it was O.K. after I died and they didn't hurt any more then.'

Unable to credit what she had just heard Irene hardly knew what to say. There were so many questions she wanted to ask her small son all at the same time that she didn't quite know where to start. Then she got the feeling that perhaps it would be better not to ask him anything at all but just to let him do the talking first and then she could follow up what he said.

Irene remembers, 'I just sat and looked at him in amazement, waiting to hear what he was going to say next. Instead of saying anything he started tucking into his bowl of custard. After a minute or two I could see that he wasn't going to continue the conversation so I thought I'd better just leave it.'

The following day Alexander was just playing around the flat as usual when Irene felt compelled to give him some kind of gentle hint just to see if he would change his story about having been killed in the war. She asked him,

'You know yesterday you told me that you had hurt your tummy and your legs? How did it happen again?' Straight away Alexander asked, 'Oh, that time when I died?' His mother nodded her head and the child went on to tell her, 'It was in the war.' She asked him, 'What war?' He replied, 'I don't know what war it was, but there was a big bang and noise and I got hurt in my tummy and legs.'

Alexander told his mother that he didn't die straight away but lived for a short time. Then the next thing he knew he was in the ground in the graveyard. 'But how did you know it was a graveyard?' asked Irene. Alexander told her, 'I knew because it was where all the people were sleeping under the ground and there were flowers on top.' Irene said, 'But if you were sleeping, how did you know that there were flowers on top?' The little boy answered, 'I was sleeping but I could see as well. I could see the roses.' Irene laughed and then asked Alexander, 'How could you see if you were sleeping? Didn't you have your eyes shut?' Alexander answered, 'Not my real eyes, Mummy. Only the ones under the ground were sleeping.'

By this time Irene was totally confused and she did not know what to think. She made an attempt to reason with her son by saying, 'Then you weren't really in the ground, were you?' He answered, 'I was in the ground but I could still walk about and see the flowers.' 'That's impossible,' said Irene. 'How could you be in two places at once?' 'You can when you're dead,' came the reply. Irene then said, 'What happened to you after that, then?' Her little boy told her that he just stayed asleep for a long time but he was able to walk around if he wanted to, although he said he felt very tired most of the time and all he wanted to do was to sleep.

Irene asked Alexander, 'Where did you walk to?' He replied, 'It wasn't really like walking, Mummy.' Irene said, 'Do you mean your legs were too sore to walk properly?' The child replied, 'They were all better when I died but I didn't have to walk on them. I was able to move without walking on my feet.' Again Irene asked her little boy where he had moved to and he told her that he had gone to see the flowers and roses on top of the grass and that he remembered going out on to the roadway. Alexander then said, 'That's how I knew the road. It's the road that Aunty Brenda brought me to.'

'Did you do anything else?' asked Irene. Alexander said, 'I used to watch the other people getting put in the ground. Lots of people got killed in the war. I used to look for their flowers on top of the grass.'

Over the following few months little Alexander often mentioned details about being killed. The story gradually emerged that he had been a grown man and that although he had been killed during one of the wars he had not been in the forces. It seems as if he had been killed in an explosion of some description – most probably by a bomb.

When he was first aware of being hurt, Alexander said that he was lying down with bricks over him. He possibly could have been trapped, the numbing weight of the bricks on top of him making him unaware of pain in his legs. 'How long were you under the bricks?' asked Irene. He answered, 'I don't know.' Then she asked him if he remembers being taken up out of the bricks and he told her, 'No, I only remember sleeping after that.' Irene said, 'You fell asleep under the bricks?' At this point there seemed to be some confusion in Alexander's mind. He wasn't sure if he was sleeping under the bricks in the place where he had been struck down or if he was sleeping in the graveyard under the ground. He is in no doubt, however, that he eventually was put under the ground and he seems to have the impression of being there for quite a while.

Then as a little test, just to see if Alexander was going to alter his story, Irene said to him, 'And that was all you can remember?' He immediately piped up, 'No. I told you I remember going out to see the flowers, remember?' Then he added, 'And I went out on to the road as well.'

'Did you see anyone on the road or talk to them?' asked Irene. 'Oh yes,' said Alexander, 'but they didn't listen to me.' Irene asked him why not and he replied, 'They just kept on walking. They didn't want to talk to me.' His mother asked him, 'Did they hear you?' The child answered, 'Oh yes, because I shouted at them, but they still didn't stop to talk to me.' 'What did you shout at them?' asked Irene. 'I told them my legs were better,' he replied. 'Weren't they glad about that?' asked his mother. Alexander just shook his head and said, 'I don't know.'

'What did you do after that?' asked Irene and Alexander replied, 'I just went back to the roses again.' His mother said, 'You mean under the ground?' 'No, I was already under the ground,' he answered. Irene said, 'But you've just told me that you had been out on the road shouting to the people. Now you're saying that you were under the ground all the time. Which is true?' Alexander explained to his mother, 'I was under the ground but that wasn't really me. I was shouting at the people.' 'After you went back to the roses did you go under the ground then?' asked Irene. Alexander replied in a somewhat weary voice, 'I didn't. I knew I was sleeping under the ground but I wanted to stay on top beside the roses.'

Irene recalls, 'He said it in such a tone of voice that he made me feel like a proper idiot not understanding what he was saying. To him it all seemed so logical and he couldn't understand why I was puzzled.'

When Alexander was about three-and-a-half his mother had him out the back in the small garden. She was talking to one of the other flat residents from the same house who shared the garden with her. The subject got round to unusual experiences and Irene just happened to mention to her neighbour some of the things that Alexander had been saying. Irene remembers, 'The woman was listening politely but with disbelief on her face, so feeling a fool I changed the subject.' Since then Irene has never discussed Alexander's memories with anyone. She says, 'It does seem so strange and ridiculous that I don't really blame people for being doubtful, but all I can say is if it happened

127

to them or someone in their own family then they would believe it.'

One day after little Alexander had been playing in the garden he went in to his mother who recalls, 'He was black as the ace of spades, just like a little boy should be.' Irene laughed. 'He looked so happy and contented and I asked him how he was doing.' He answered, 'Fine,' and then he added, 'And if I'm extra good in this life then I'll be given another chance in my next life.' Brenda who was in the flat with Irene at the time said, 'I nearly turned green when I heard him. He was only a tiny nipper and I just couldn't understand how he could know to say a thing like that.'

As Alexander grew older his memories faded out until by the time he started school he remembered nothing at all about his previous life. One day Irene told him about the things he used to say when he was a baby and he got very embarrassed and said that he couldn't remember any of that. The only thing that did linger on in his mind was the feeling that he had been killed in a war.

When he was six, he went up to Irene one day and whispered that he wanted to tell her something. She asked what it was and he said, 'Promise you won't laugh at me, and say I'm silly.' Irene promised but she was intrigued and thought to herself that he was probably going to tell her that he had a girlfriend.

Alexander said to his mother, 'Mummy, I think I died in a war, but I don't know what war.' Irene remembers that all his childish ramblings came back to her. Since that remark Alexander has not mentioned anything else.

Irene wonders if her son really had wandered across Willesden Lane cemetery and if he had tried to communicate with the people hurrying past him on the roadway that day. Every so often she used to walk down that road and she could never resist glancing across at the graveyard and wondering, although she never dared venture in.

Girl remembers watching silversmith at work

Mandy Richards, *Llandyfyl*

When Mandy was two years old her aunt moved from Wales to Norfolk, which was brand new territory for the whole family. After a few weeks of settling in, Mandy's mother Sybal received an invitation to go and visit her sister at the new house, so one bright summer afternoon Mandy set off with her mother and father on the long drive from Wales.

The journey was pleasant and the family stopped for lunch on the way. The roads were not too busy and Mandy's father was able to enjoy the drive. On the outskirts of the town of Harleston, a place completely unknown to the family, Mandy suddenly yelled out excitedly, 'Oh look, Mummy, that's where the old man made all the rings.' The child was pointing to an old derelict shack with a black tarmac roof. Her parents just fobbed the child off thinking that she was just half dreaming, but Mandy persisted, saying, 'I remember watching him through the window.'

Sybal asked her little girl, 'What man, Mandy?' and the child replied, 'The old man with the funny hammer.' Sybal was sure that the child was thinking about some toy hammer or that perhaps she had heard a story about a man with a hammer, so she said, 'Are you thinking of someone from your story books, love?' Mandy shook her head and said, 'No, Mummy. It was a real man. I used to watch him through the window round the back.' Sybal asked her, 'When was this, love?' knowing perfectly well that her daughter had never even been out of Wales before and could not possibly have been to the old shack. Mandy answered, 'When I lived before, and I used to look in the back window.'

Mandy's father started to become interested in the

conversation when he heard the child say such a strange thing. He asked his daughter, 'How could you have lived before, Mandy?' and the child told him, 'Oh I remember it. I lived near here and I used to play around the hut with my sister.'

Her parents laughed when they heard this and Sybal said, 'But you don't have a sister, Mandy.' The child replied, 'No, but I did have when I lived before.' Mandy then went on to tell her parents that she remembers having had a sister called Sarah, although she could not remember what her own name had been. Sarah had been a few years older than Mandy and when they used to play around the old shack the bigger girl would lift Mandy up so that she could peep in through the back window. Mandy says, 'I saw an old man with a funny hammer thing. He was bashing away at silver rings and bracelets on a workbench.' She vividly remembers the man's face. He never used to take any notice of her. He had grey hair and a grey bushy moustache, and he wore thin-rimmed spectacles which had very small lenses in them. Mandy remembers that the man wore the glasses perched on the end of his nose as he looked down through them on to his workbench.

Mandy told her parents how the small window at the back of the shed was, as she put it, 'in two halves. The bottom half was cloudy glass that I couldn't see through but the top half was just ordinary glass. That's why Sarah had to lift me up so that I could see in through the top half of the window.' She said that as well as the old man there were two or three other people working in the shed, all ladies, and all doing something to the rings. She thought that one lady was always packing the silverware up into little boxes, then wrapping them up with brown paper.

The man was the clearest in Mandy's memory because he had been working at his bench facing the window. His work seemed to alternate from banging wildly at the pieces of silver with his peculiar-looking hammer, to doing more intricate detailed work, because Mandy described him as sometimes being very serious as if he was concentrating very hard on the item before him on the bench.

She doesn't recall any details about the women or their clothes or hairstyles but she does remember that the man was all dressed in dark colours. He wore a shirt or jumper of either black or dark navy-blue and over this he had on a large black leather apron. She remembers thinking how strange his hands looked.

Each and every time the family would visit that particular part of the country, Mandy would say the same thing. She always pointed to the same shack and she always said that she had watched the old man making rings when she had lived before.

This had been going on for about a year when Sybal decided that it was about time that she put a stop to what she thought were her little girl's imaginative wanderings. One day when they were driving towards her sister's house she asked her husband to stop the car at the shack so that they could walk around it with Mandy just to prove to her that the back of it was nothing like she had described, and so put the matter out of her head once and for all.

They got out and walked round the back of the old tumbledown shack and sure enough there was the one window at the back in the exact position that Mandy had described. Sybal says, 'It was so old I knew that it probably hadn't been used for years.' The window had been barred across on the outside with thick iron bars which were coated in rust, but behind these, through the thick layers of dust and cobwebs, Sybal could see the old glass window still intact. She gasped when she realized that the lower half of the window was fitted with dull frosted glass, while in the top half there was the ordinary clear variety. Immediately she remembered that little Mandy had described the lower half of the window as cloudy and that she could not see through it. The child was too young to know the term frosted but she had certainly got the description correct.

When they looked into the shed they could see that it was filled up with old junk. Sybal says, 'It looked as if it had been used as a storage shed at one time but everything inside looked so rusty and old I got the impression that the owner had just gone off and forgotten all about the place.'

The shack still stands to this day, just outside Harleston near an old disused railway bridge. Mandy's parents wonder if there ever has been a silversmith who worked in the old shack, but Mandy doesn't wonder, she says she knows there was, because she saw him working with his hammer.

Although Mandy cannot remember anything much about her previous parents she has flashes in her mind that they used to visit a friend's house somewhere near the old shack. It was on these occasions that Mandy and her sister used to watch the old man at work.

Unbeknown to Mandy or Sybal, further research was carried out to see if there has ever been a silversmith who worked in that area. From the census offices in Norwich we received confirmation that in the year 1868 there did indeed exist a silversmith who had his own little business just on the outskirts of Harleston. At that time the area was virtually open country and the way in which isolated houses or huts were documented was by relating them to the nearest railway line. The silversmith, a Mr Michael Mothersole, was believed to have operated from a location very close to where the road was crossed by the railway line by an old iron bridge. This is the precise spot where the old shack still stands to this day.

Girl remembers being a nun

Elspeth Lacey, *Newcastle*

When Elspeth had only just started to talk at around eighteen months her mother was bathing her one night when she started mumbling away to herself in the bath. Her mother got the impression that the little girl was trying very hard to communicate, but because the child had only just started to put phrases together she was obviously finding it difficult to say exactly what was in her mind.

Her mother asked her to repeat herself and she said quite clearly, 'I'm going to the vows.' Elspeth's mother asked her, 'The vows? Where's the vows?' The child answered, 'You know, the vows up the big hill.' At this point Elspeth's eyes glazed over and she appeared to be in some kind of trance. Her mother Joan says, 'The strange look on her face sent shivers up my spine. She was in a complete daze.'

Elspeth went on to tell her mother that she was on her way up the hill to the vows. There were lots of flowers around her, growing by the side of the footpath. She said, 'We like to pick the flowers for the altar.' Joan asked her little girl where she was going and Elspeth answered, 'I'm going to take my vows with the other girls.' When her mother heard Elspeth phrase the words in that way it began to make sense to her. She asked the little girl, 'What vows are you going to take, Elspeth?' The answer came back, 'I'm not Elspeth now.' Her mother gently asked her who she was and the little girl said, 'I'm Rose, but I'm going to be Sister Teresa Gregory.'

Joan was fascinated by her daughter's words, both at the way she was speaking coherently and at the content of her story. She knew that the child had no knowledge of nuns or vows or anything like that. She says, 'We have no nuns in the family at all, in fact we're not even Catholics. I was dumbfounded when she started talking as if she knew all about being a nun.'

Elspeth then told her mother, 'I've got a long frock on and I'm walking up to the altar. I've got my white frock on.' After that, Elspeth gave a little jump and she looked up at her mother Joan and stared at her. Joan says, 'She looked so startled as if she had suddenly wakened up.' Joan got her little daughter out of the bath and started dressing her for bed. Just as she was snuggling down under her covers with her teddy bear Elspeth said to her mother, 'Do you know that I was an old lady once, Mummy?' Joan asked her what she meant and she answered, 'I always had a long black dress down to the ground and I had a black cloth over my head and I was very very old.' Joan asked her where she was when she was old and Elspeth replied, 'It was when I was here before.'

Joan could see that Elspeth was getting very sleepy so she didn't want her to go on talking much longer. She tried to settle the child down, but Elspeth seemed to be once more in her trance. Joan says, 'She just lay in her bed staring up blankly at the ceiling. Normally she would look at my face when she talked to me, but not this time. She had the same glazed look in her eyes that I had seen when she was in the bath.'

The child said nothing more that night and for a long time there were no other such occurrences. Joan had almost forgotten all about her daughter's story about being old and having had a previous life till one night about two years later when Elspeth was four she was chatting normally to her mother when her eyes suddenly glazed over again and she began to talk.

The child's words came pouring out without any effort or hesitation. She said that she had been a nun and that the convent was in a country area where there were lots of flowers. She remembered when she first went to the convent as a novice and then later took her final vows. As a nun, Elspeth, or Sister Teresa Gregory as she was known, had to do lots of jobs around the convent. She had to milk goats and help cook the food and make cheese. She said that she wasn't allowed to talk very much especially when a certain bell was rung. It was the sign that the nuns were to keep silent no matter what they were doing.

She remembered that she used to say a lot of prayers and that she lived in a tiny cell with only a bed and one or two other pieces of furniture in it. The child described it as cold and she said that she had to get up very early in the morning, sometimes when it was still dark.

Elspeth stopped speaking for a while. Joan did not feel comfortable leaving the child until she was sure that her daughter was completely back to normal and out of the dazed state. Joan says, 'Although she had stopped talking I felt that she was still deep in her trance because her eyes were still quite glassy-looking. I wasn't quite sure what to do. I didn't want to shake her or anything in case she was startled. She seemed very happy and she had such a peaceful expression on her face. I decided that I'd better say something to her to see if that would bring her back to normal.'

'Are you feeling all right?' asked Joan. Elspeth replied, 'Yes.' Joan says, 'When I asked her that, it seemed to set her off again because she went on to tell me how she died.' Elspeth told her mother that she had been praying in her room and she fell down on to the floor. She remembers trying to call out but couldn't. The next thing she knew was that everything went dark.

From out of the darkness, Elspeth woke up to find that some of her friends were with her. They told her that she would be going to stay with them for a while. She said that these friends were also nuns who had died before her. They all had their nuns' habits on but some of them looked younger than she had remembered them. Then Elspeth said that after a while she started to get young again too. She said that she waited with her nuns for a while only;

then she went away to live somewhere else. She did not seem to have any memories after this point.

Joan says, 'She was talking like someone who had been hypnotized. I didn't ask her any questions except that one about how she was feeling and she just kept talking all the time, without any prompting from me. I just sat quietly and listened.' Joan says that when her little girl got to the part where she had left the other nuns to go away to a different place, it was almost as if everything in her mind faded out. It was only then that she caught her mother's eye and Joan realized that Elspeth had started to focus properly again.

Since then there have been no more trances or remarks about being a nun. Elspeth is now a happy playful little seven-year-old girl who loves her school and joins in with all the games in a carefree way. Her mother says, 'Sometimes when I see her tearing around with her little friend's football I find it very hard to imagine her as a nun. Still, her memories seemed very real at the time, and considering how young she was I can't believe that she could have picked it up from anywhere, especially since the first time she mentioned about the vows she was practically a baby, hardly able to talk at all.'

Joan has never told Elspeth what she used to say when she was younger. She feels that her little girl has probably forgotten all about it. Meanwhile Elspeth plays football with her friend from next door. Joan says, 'She doesn't bother much with dolls and girls' toys, she seems much more interested in trying to score goals at football!' Then Joan adds with a laugh, 'She's a right little tomboy.'

Girl remembers pet horse from previous life

Debbie Sellers, *Hornsea*

Ever since she was a baby, Debbie has always had what her mother Sandra describes as 'an uncanny way with horses'. Her mother could never quite understand this as she herself was always terrified of horses.

One night when Debbie was three years old, her mother put her to bed as usual, but just before the child dropped off to sleep, Sandra heard chuckles of laughter coming from Debbie's bedroom. When her mother went to see what was causing the mirth, Debbie told her, 'Oh I was just thinking about the time when I was riding my horse over fields and I came to a roadway and on the road there was a policeman on a bicycle. I went past him and put my arm out and knocked his hat off. He was very angry but I galloped off quickly and couldn't help laughing.'

Debbie's mother asked her when all this happened, and the child replied, 'Oh when I lived before.' She told her mother, 'We owned lots of horses and I loved them all. Paintbrush was my special horse. He was brown with patches on him.'

Debbie remembers how she used to help her husband in the stables. She described to her mother how to saddle, bridle and groom a horse, although she has never owned or ridden a horse in her life. Debbie tells of how she lived in the country and her husband ran a kind of riding school. She says, 'Lots of children and some adults used to come to ride our horses, and my husband showed them what to do.' Then she added, 'But I knew how to gallop on Paintbrush because he already showed me.' She was responsible for looking after Paintbrush.

When Sandra asked Debbie if she went to school the child replied, 'Oh yes. It was in the village.' She said she liked school and has remembered some of the things she was taught in her previous school. Recently Debbie started school, and when she had been there for a while her teacher gave her some simple spelling to learn. She always got every one of the spellings correct and when Sandra remarked to the child that she had never seen her learning them at home, Debbie replied, 'Why learn what I already know? I've already done all those words a long time ago.'

Although Debbie is aware of having been part of a family in her previous life, she can only recall her husband. She said his name had been something like Davidson. Then she added, 'But maybe it was just David.' She is not clear whether the David is part of the surname or whether it had been her husband's Christian name. She has no recollection of the rest of her family but she seems to think that there were quite a few people involved, although she does not know if they were brothers, sisters or other relatives.

Her main memories centre round the horses. She says, 'I loved it when I gave Paintbrush his dinner. He got it from a big bag of stuff.' Sandra thinks that Debbie's previous family may have been horse breeders because her daughter remembers, 'There were always lots of new baby horses but I didn't get to ride them.'

Debbie remembers the house that she used to live in as being old with big rooms and a very large kitchen. Sandra says, 'It sounds like a very old farmhouse by the way Debbie describes it.' The kitchen seems to stick in the child's mind more than any other part of the house. She says, 'It had a funny black shiny oven that was attached to the fire.' Apparently when the fire was lit the heat would spread to the oven part and in this way the food could be cooked. It must have been rather antiquated because there doesn't seem to have been any gas or electricity. Sometimes pots and kettles were placed on top of the fire, literally amid the burning cinders, and sometimes they would be hung over the flames from some kind of extended hook.

Another thing that Debbie remembers about the kitchen

was that it had a large marble slab which was used as a work-top for baking bread. The loaves of bread would then be placed in the black oven to cook. Debbie says, 'I remember the lovely smell of the bread in our kitchen.'

Debbie's father Jim, a very practical kiln manager, is highly intrigued by his little girl's memories. He says, 'Well, she's either got a vivid imagination or else she's lived before.' Then he added with a laugh, 'I wouldn't like to put my money on it either way.'

As for Debbie, her big ambition is to own a horse again. Her father says, 'She's supposed to be saving up to buy one just like Paintbrush, but the way she's going she'll be a pensioner before she makes it. Every time the ice-cream van passes the door she's out like a shot to spend her money. Then she's got to start saving all over again.'

Boy remembers waiting to be reborn

Daniel Jones, *Preston*

Two-and-a-half year old Daniel is a beautiful brown-eyed dark-haired child with a ready smile. The great love of his life is water. He adores his bath and usually cries when his mother picks him up out of it to dry him off.

On odd occasions when Daniel has been brought to the sea-side he has been entranced by the sight of the sea. His mother Greta remembers the very first time her boy saw the sea at Blackpool. She says, 'I thought his eyes were going to pop out of his head he got so excited. He just couldn't wait to get his swimming trunks on. Although he was excited, I thought that he might be just a bit timid of actually going into the water for the first time, so I told him that I would take his hand and go in with him, but I never got the chance. He was off like a bee as fast as he could go, straight for the water. I ran after him expecting him to stop when he got to the water's edge but instead he ran straight in and started dancing up and down with sheer joy.'

When he was eventually persuaded to come out of the water, Daniel said the strangest thing to his mother who was busy with a towel trying to dry him off. He said, 'I had to go into the water to get born, Mummy.' His mother was so taken up with getting her child dry she didn't pay too much attention to him and just made a casual reply, 'Oh that was nice,' without really thinking about what she was saying.

Daniel then said, 'It wasn't the same as the sea, though. It was a river.' Again Greta answered automatically, saying, 'Oh really? Where was that, love?' Daniel answered, 'It was in Heaven, of course.' Greta's ears started to prick when she heard this, and she asked Daniel, 'What are you on about, Danny?' Her son then said, 'You know, Heaven, where all the little boys and girls live before they get to be born.'

By now Greta was beginning to be interested in this strange conversation, so she said, 'Well, where is this Heaven then?' The child answered, 'It's where the river was before I was born.' Greta became more and more intrigued as she listened to her son. She asked him, 'How do you know that it was Heaven?' and he replied, 'Well that's the name everybody here gives it.' His mother asked him, 'Is that the name you called it when you were there?' The child replied, 'No.' Greta asked him what he had called it then, and he told her that they didn't call it anything, they just lived there.

As the weeks and months went past, every now and then Daniel would remember more and more details about his life in this other place where he lived before he was born. When he was nearly four he told his mother that there were lots of other children there and they were all good friends. The river flowed through this place and when it was time for any of the children to be born they would be led to the river with all their friends around them and then they would either jump into the water themselves or else someone would push them in.

Daniel remembers very well when it was his turn to be born. He said that he had been told well in advance that he would soon be leaving all his friends for a while because he was to come to Earth and that his Mummy and Daddy would be waiting for him. He was told that he would see his friends again when he went back there to live with them all again.

A strange thing that Daniel said was that he knows some of his friends were going to be born at the same time as he was and they all knew that they would meet up with each other while they lived on earth. When his mother asked him if he knew any of these friends Daniel told her that he hadn't met them yet, but he was sure that as soon as he did meet one of them they would know each other straightaway. When Greta asked Daniel if he knew his friends' names he told her that their names would all be different on earth but the little boy was confident that somehow he would know his friends when they eventually met.

Daniel said that when it was his turn to be born he was pushed into the river and that was all he could remember. He went on to tell Greta that when he went into the river, that was the time when he left the other place where he had been living. He told his mother, 'That's when I came to you and Daddy.'

Greta and her husband Ralph can't help wondering if their little boy really does remember living in what we think of as Heaven. They find it so hard to believe that he could have thought up such an involved story. All his statements seemed to be so spontaneous.

Daniel is a well-behaved child who is thoughtful and considerate. Greta says, 'Sometimes I think that he's so much wiser than I am. It's funny, but the way he looks at me sometimes, I feel that there is so much in his eyes that he wants to tell me.'

Girl remembers being hit by previous mother

Mandy Hartley, *Maidstone*

From the moment she was born Mandy was an alert bright baby, very aware of everything which was going on around her. Her mother Susan says, 'The minute she was born she was handed over to me. I took her in my arms and she not only opened her eyes and focused on me but she actually seemed to look at me and say, "Who are you?" '

During the following few days in hospital Susan was constantly amazed at the reactions of her new-born baby. The infant seemed to understand everything which was being said to her. Her mother remembers, 'She had such a knowing look on her face as if she already knew the whole routine of babyhood back to front.' Susan remembers that when her mother-in-law came to the hospital to see the baby for the first time she took one look at Mandy and said 'You're foxy, you've been on this earth before.'

One day when she was two-and-a-half years old, Mandy got up to some childish mischief in the kitchen. Susan came in to find the child sitting in the middle of the floor covered from head to toe in cream, surrounded by half-a-dozen half-eaten cakes from which she had eaten all the cream apart from that which was mashed into her hair and smudged all over her clothes, face and arms. Susan's immediate reaction was to burst into laughter but when the laughter subsided, she thought about the cakes and naturally enough she was rather cross. She attempted to tell the child off and was just about to try to make the little girl understand that stealing cakes was not a very lady-like thing to do, when Mandy, being well aware that her mother was annoyed and sensing that she was going to be told off, chirped up, 'I'm going to tell my mummy of you.'

Susan was stopped in her tracks at the child's words. 'But I am your mummy,' she said. Mandy answered, 'I mean my other mummy.' Her mother asked her what she meant, and Mandy replied, 'My mummy when I was a little girl before.' Susan told her, 'You weren't a little girl before. What on earth are you talking about?' The child replied, 'Oh yes I was, and I had another mummy.'

Susan could see that Mandy was absolutely serious so she asked her, 'Well, why did you leave your other mummy then?' A rather dejected expression crept over the child's face. Then she answered, 'Because she hit me with knives.' Susan was horrified, and she asked her daughter, 'Are you sure? Are you just making all this up, Mandy?' Mandy said, 'She did hit me with knives and then I died.' Mandy looked quite upset by this time so Susan thought it best to change the subject.

Some weeks later when Mandy was in bed she again mentioned her other mummy to Susan. This time the child went on to talk about her death. She said, 'I was very poorly. Then I feel asleep and went very small. I woke up and I was with you and Daddy and then I grew big again, into a big girl.' Susan asked Mandy if she knew what age she was when she was poorly and the child replied, 'I think I was eight.'

Mandy then told her mother that she remembered the time just before she was born. She said, 'I was in your tummy. It was when I woke up again.' She told her mother that it was dark and warm and she could hear outside noises, and that she had heard Susan talking and sometimes shouting.

When Mandy was only two years old, Susan unfortunately had a miscarriage in the tenth week of her pregnancy. Soon afterwards she conceived again and Mandy informed her mother that although the earlier baby had died in her tummy the very same baby had come back to her.

Susan is not certain what to think of her child's remarks. She is very open-minded on the subject of reincarnation and says, 'I can't say for sure whether my little girl really has lived before. Who can really tell? Her memories just seem to come in flashes now and again. There's no way to really prove anything but at the same time when she does get these flashes they come so quickly. She blurts out things without taking time to work anything out in advance.'

The girl has mentioned her other mummy so often that Susan feels there could well be something behind all of Mandy's remarks if it was possible to dig deep enough, although she doesn't wish to have her child hypnotized or anything like that. She says, 'It's the expression on her face more than anything else that is so convincing. There's no doubt in my mind that she believes her memories to be real, so who knows?'

Two-year-old girl remembers being born

Hermione Baker, *London*

Little Hermione, named after her godmother, a famous actress, has distinct memories of her own birth. She describes it to her mother Anne as being very noisy and tiring. In the child's own baby words, 'When I were born it were very dark and I heard loud noises. I felt very tired.'

Hermione says that before she was born she was with Jesus. She says, 'But He went away. I did not know where He was going and He didn't say.'

She remembers the days and months before her birth when she existed in her mother's womb, and her conscious memory goes back even further than that to a previous life in which two little boys were her special friends.

According to Hermione, the darkness which she experienced during her birth did not exist while she was in her mother's womb waiting to be born, but she does remember the sounds of the outside world penetrating into the womb. She says, 'It were golden and bright, but noisy like chug chug,' and she says that she could hear her mother speaking.

One day while Hermione's actress mother was busy looking over one of her scripts, Hermione suddenly announced, 'I'm in my life.' Her mother was quite amazed. Then the child followed this up with, 'I'm in the whole world.' Anne says that the statements seemed to come out of the blue, and were not preceded by any other conversation. She seemed to be in a state of wonderment and great happiness.

Maps hold a strange fascination for Hermione and she appears to have an inner knowledge of geography. The first time she ever saw a map was in January 1982 when her mother came across an old map of the world which had been folded away in a drawer. In an attempt to keep her daughter amused for a time, Anne thought that she would show the map to Hermione to let the child see what the world really looks like. She spread the map out on the coffee table, but before she had time to say a word, Hermione pointed to North America and said, 'That America. Godmama lives there.' Her godmother does indeed live in New York. Anne then pointed to Kenya on the map and straight away Hermione said, 'That in Africa.' Anne was overwhelmed at this because she had never mentioned the word Africa.

About a month after the map incident, Anne was reading *Alice in Wonderland* to her daughter. Anne recalls, 'She was listening intently, but I couldn't believe she was really understanding it. After I read, "The caterpillar was smoking a hookah", I asked her if she knew what a hookah was. Very confidently Hermione replied, "I do." ' Somewhat sceptically Anne asked her, 'What is it, then?' Hermione replied, 'It a pipe,' as if she was amazed at her mother's ignorance.

Anne describes herself as an agnostic, and very sceptical about reincarnation but she admits that Hermione's insight into things which belies her age really makes her wonder.

Hermione's father, a solicitor, is open-minded on the subject. He is a practising member of the Anglican Church and like his wife Anne he is not given to assumptions. He does not know quite what to make of Hermione's statements. Anne says that her husband is just not sure what lies behind it all. 'It takes a lot to really convince him about such matters, but in spite of himself, he feels that there is definitely something strange about the way our little girl knows so many things that she has never been taught.'

Normally Anne buys frozen peas, but one day she was passing a greengrocer's shop and she caught sight of some pea-pods. She thought that it might be a good idea to buy some and take them home to Hermione to show her how to do some podding. Anne says, 'It was to give her something to do more than anything else.' To Anne, podding peas seemed like a marvellous change from the never-ending rows of sticky dough messes which little Hermione proudly referred to as 'my cakes ready to go in the oven'.

Anne took the peas out of the bag and was all set to explain to Hermione what they were, as she knew that the child had never seen peas in a pod before, but before she had time to utter a word the child chirped up, 'Oh goody, pea-pods! I haven't done podding for a long time.' Anne knows for a fact that Hermione has never done podding at all.

The child said, 'I need a colander when I do podding.' This tickled her mother because the word colander was totally outside the child's vocabulary. 'I had no idea that she had even heard the word, or knew what a colander was used for, but she put her little apron on, rolled up her sleeves and set to work as if she had been doing it all her life. She knew exactly what to do without my having to say a single word.'

One day Hermione was chatting away happily with her mother about some of her friends. She was relating a story about some funny incident that had recently occurred. Anne asked Hermione if she had made friends with any boys. The following is the resulting conversation which took place between Hermione and Anne:

Hermione: (In reply to her mother's question about making friends with boys) I haven't. I have. Those little boys have already died. Have already died from me.

Anne: Cried?

Hermione: Died.

Anne: Who's died?

Hermione: Those little boys who I had made friends with. Those two boys.

Anne: You made friends with two little boys?

Hermione: And those have already died.

Anne: The friendships died?

Hermione: No.

Anne: No?

Hermione: Those little boys who I did make friends with.

Anne: What's happened to them?

Hermione: Died.

Anne: How did they die?

Hermione: They did fall into the water and a shark did eat them.

Anne: Oh dear! So they won't be coming anymore?

Hermione: No.

Anne: Who told you about this?

Hermione: None of the little boys – none.

Anne: Is that a true story?

Hermione: Mmm.

Anne: Have you seen them since this?

Hermione: Mmm. A shark did come and eat they up and I saw they go in and I didn't fall in.

Anne: Is this when you were swimming?

Hermione: No.

Anne: Oh, I think you're making all this up!

Anne says that she is loathe to question Hermione outright for obvious reasons, but because of the odd flashes of past memories the child experiences, she thought that she would ask a few test questions just to see what her daughter's reaction would be.

The following is an account of the experiment. Anne wonders whether it is all just a delightful babble of nonsense or if there is more to it than that. 'I'm not really sure what to make of it,' says Anne. 'I noticed she seems to have a recurring fascination with sharks, although she has never seen a real one.'

Anne: I don't really believe it but some people think they've lived before. Do you think you have?

Hermione: I do.

Anne: Where did you live?

Hermione: In London.

Anne: When? Now?

Hermione: Long ago.

Anne: What did you wear?

Hermione: Like this. (She was wearing a short white dress.)

Anne: Just the same? or longer?

Hermione: Longer.

Anne: Who were you?

Hermione: I was a lady.

Anne: A lady of *Leisure*?

Hermione: I was a lady of *Pleasure* (!)

Anne: Were you married?

Hermione: I was.

Anne: Did you have any children?

Hermione: I did.

Anne: How many?

Hermione: 16-17.

Anne: Did you live in London all the time?

Hermione: In London and Northland. (No great break-through. Northland comes into *Noggin the Nog*.)

Anne: And what were you in Northland?

Hermione: I was half a man and half a woman and I was on a boat and I was eaten by a shark!

Hermione's mother Anne, a well-known West End actress, is rather non-committal regarding her daughter's memories of far-off lives and sharks. 'Who really knows what it is?' she says.

Hermione is a healthy happy toddler, somewhat chubby and extremely pretty with big blue eyes and fair straight short hair. 'She loves her food,' remarks her mother, 'and she will eat positively anything including our best Stilton cheese. She is a darling little girl and a great delight to us.'

Anne remembers when Hermione was only a year old and she took her into their local post office to buy some stamps. While they were waiting in the queue a perfect stranger walked up to Anne, and pointing to the baby said, 'That one has been here before. Look at her face. She's seen it all.' Anne says, 'I didn't take much notice of it at the time, but so many little incidents make me wonder.'

Life After Death

There are countless cases of people who have given evidence of survival after death; indeed so many that the subject is well catered for in the many volumes of books which adorn the shelves of our public libraries up and down the country. However in the course of our own research into life before birth, several interesting experiences have been brought to our notice which substantiate the case for survival of the personality after physical death.

As our research dealt primarily with children, the case histories dealt with in this chapter also feature babies or young children, and we feel sure that we should include these accounts in this book, not only for their interest value, but because we sincerely believe that the stories will bring some degree of solace to bereaved parents and offer them a hope to cling to that they will eventually be re-united with their children.

Mrs Angela Rigg-Milner, a doctor's wife, is a very sensible, level-headed lady, very down to earth and not given to flights of fancy. One day Angela was driving along the arterial road at East Horndon, Southend, when her car was involved in a three-vehicle smash. Five-year-old Samantha, the youngest of Angela's three children, sustained critical head injuries, and three days later the child died.

Angela was inconsolable, and at the time had no religious beliefs. Despite the bitter heart-break Angela experienced at the time of Samantha's death she refused to take any pills which would have dulled her senses. She knew that somehow or other she was going to have to get through the ordeal by herself, without resorting to drugs or alcohol. She was tortured by feelings of guilt and she kept blaming herself for her daughter's death, telling herself that if she hadn't taken the children out for that car run it might never have happened.

She tried desperately to come to terms with the situation and she made a brave effort to face up to life for the sake of her husband and her other two children. She knew how much they were all suffering already, and she didn't want to add to their unhappiness by having a break-down. Being a doctor's wife, she was well aware of the dangers of depression and she made up her mind to do her best just to keep going in the face of her grief and desolation.

Then an extraordinary thing happened which entirely changed the course of Angela's life. She had been walking through the house one night, just six weeks after Samantha had died, unable to sleep, feeling restless and uneasy. She went back to bed and she noticed that the time was 5.30 a.m. by the clock on her teamaker. Something made her turn and look towards her dressing table which is incorporated into a unit in the corner of the bedroom. 'There was Samantha, standing in the bedroom watching me,' says Angela. 'She was wearing her favourite pink-and-white nightgown.' Angela had not allowed Samantha to wear that particular nightgown very much because it was made of nylon. She knew the nightgown was folded in the drawer in the children's room, but yet there was Samantha wearing it.

Angela says, 'She looked extremely bewildered and lost. I got out of bed and walked down to the end of it and sat down, watching Samantha all the time. She was now only about two-and-a-half feet away from me.'

Then Angela spoke to her daughter. 'Hello, darling,' she said. 'You're not dead at all, are you?' Samantha replied, 'I'm very tired, Mummy.' Angela says, 'I put out my arms and she walked over to me. It was the most unbelievable thing anyone could imagine. She sat on my knee and she was warm and solid and very much alive. I stroked her long silky hair and she felt real in every way, just like any normal child.'

Angela was completely aware that something remarkable was taking place and she made a point of lifting up one of Samantha's arms to make sure that it was real. She says, 'Her arm felt warm and perfectly normal. I touched her body from head to toe and it was every bit as complete and solid as you and me.'

Angela then asked Samantha if she would like to come into bed beside Mummy and Daddy for a cuddle. At this point, Angela called her husband so that he too could see Samantha, but she just couldn't waken him up. She says, 'I was afraid to call him too loudly for fear that the noise or disturbance would make Samantha go. When he didn't wake up I thought I'd better leave him.' She then took Samantha by the hand and walked round the side of the bed and took the child into bed with her.

Angela says, 'She snuggled in to me quite naturally, the way she always had done. Again I stroked her long brown hair as it spread across the pillow, and it felt just as ordinary as ever.'

After a few minutes Samantha said, 'I am tired. I've got to go now, Mummy.' Angela could see that as Samantha said the words she was looking into the corner of the room to the spot where she had first appeared. She says, 'It was as if Samantha was looking at someone, and being told to come back. I could see nothing there at all, but I'm certain that my daughter was following someone's guidance.'

Angela then asked her little girl, 'Will you come back and see Mummy again?' but the child didn't answer. Angela says, 'The next second she just disappeared. I immediately looked at the clock by the bed and it was exactly 5.40 a.m. The whole thing had lasted for ten minutes.'

Angela vividly remembers her feelings at that moment. 'I felt an unbelievable sense of relief that I will never forget. Out of the hell came this incredible peace, with the knowledge that life does exist after death.'

The experience has changed Angela's entire outlook on

life. She explains, 'I admit I used to be a very materialistic person and had no real religious beliefs, but since seeing Samantha after she died I now know for sure that life continues. It was inevitable that I should change my opinions drastically.'

Angela now devotes her life to helping other parents of children who have died. She is a member of an organization called 'Compassionate Friends' which was set up by a group of bereaved parents. Members are on call day and night to offer help and sympathy to those in mourning.

A famous American medium once told Angela that she had shared a previous life with Samantha and that the child had been meant to die so that Angela would later be shown the proof of survival after death.

'The relationship was not a parent-child one,' says Angela. 'We were just friends in our previous lives. Seemingly there was a debt owed to me by Samantha in repayment for some good turn which I had done for her. The manner in which this debt was repaid was carefully worked out so that I would be led to change my ideas and opinions, and indeed my whole way of life. Samantha was to be born to me as a daughter, then die and then return, leaving me in no doubt as to the fact that life does continue after death.

'It may seem a harsh way to prove a point,' says Angela, 'but I suppose it was the only way ever to convince someone like me that there is more to life than the materialistic side. I was such a sceptic.'

Angela says that she now thanks Samantha for the experience because she is so much richer in spirit for having gone through the ordeal. She now believes, where before she didn't. She feels that Samantha is always with her and she knows that they can never be truly separated.

Debbie Neesden lost her baby in a cot death when he was only a few months old. For the first week after the child died, his mother's grief was almost unbearable. Then something happened which helped to console her and lighten the weight of her agony.

She explains, 'A week after my baby died, I had a strange dream. A woman appeared seemingly from nowhere with a small bundle in her arms. I could not see her face as it was veiled by light but I knew she was holding my baby boy. I could see that his hair was definitely the same shape round his forehead.' In the dream Debbie went up to the woman, who did not speak but pulled back the shawl and showed Debbie her baby. Debbie asked the woman to give her the baby, and the woman reluctantly agreed. Debbie took the infant, held him tightly and kissed him over and over again.

Debbie says, 'I then asked the woman if I could take the baby away with me, but she shook her head, held out her arms and took my son away from me. At this point I woke up and found myself in tears.'

A month later Debbie had another dream in which she was walking about in a large storeroom which was filled with big crates. She heard a noise, turned round and found herself face-to-face with the same unknown woman who had appeared to her in her previous dream. Debbie remembers, 'Our eyes met and she beckoned me to follow her, which I did, and she led me round the back of some crates, stopped by one, and invited me to look inside. I did so and there lying in the crate was my baby son. He looked a lot older than he was at the time of his death. He looked like a baby of about seven months and he was much bigger than I expected. He recognized me and held out his hands.'

Just when Debbie was about to pick up the baby, the woman shook her head, picked him up herself and started to walk away with him. This upset Debbie so much that she screamed after the woman to stop, but the woman didn't. Debbie then ran after her but she kept darting in and out behind the big crates to avoid her, till Debbie yelled out, 'Why tease me like this? I only want to hold him.' Then the woman disappeared and Debbie woke up feeling extremely distressed.

Several weeks later she had the most interesting dream of all. She found herself outside a shopping precinct and recognized her pram outside a shop. She went up to the pram, looked inside, and there was her lovely baby lying in the pram chatting to himself. Again he recognized Debbie and smiled up at her. She says, 'He seemed to be roughly the same age as before. The same woman then came out of the shop and she smiled at me. I knew she was the woman from the other two dreams, but there was something more familiar than that about her. I had the feeling that I knew her from somewhere, but I couldn't think who she might be. She was about seventy years old and had white hair. I stroked my baby's head and he cooed at me, and I began to cry. The woman held me to her and told me not to cry because she said that she was looking after him now and that he was very happy with her.'

The woman explained to Debbie that soon these dreams would stop and that she would not see her baby any more, but that everything would be explained to her in her next dream. Debbie accepted this, kissed her baby and then woke up. This time she felt far more relaxed and was not upset or frustrated as she had been the time before. She was just a little perturbed by the fact that her baby had not cried to be with her.

Debbie had the final dream about five months later. She found herself on a grass verge by a shallow stream. There was a bridge over the water, and she saw a woman and a child walking over the bridge and approaching her. The child was a beautiful fair-haired little boy who was holding on to the woman's hand. Debbie remembers that as they came nearer to her, she noticed that the child was very unsteady on his feet, as if he had only just learnt to walk.

Debbie says, 'When they came up close to me I recognized them both. It was my darling baby Lee

Michael John, and the woman was my beloved grandmother who had died ten years previously.'

'I grabbed my son, who cuddled me closely,' says Debbie. 'He looked about a year old. He wore ordinary clothes, just like any other small boy would wear in summertime, and chatted away in his own style.'

Debbie's grandmother told her that Lee Michael John was a good child and that he was not meant to have been born to earthly parents, but was meant to be a spirit child. The old lady went on to explain to Debbie that although her heart had been broken it was all for the best, because if the baby hadn't died of a cot death when he did, God would have called him just before his third birthday. Debbie was told that soon she would conceive again and give birth to a female child.

The woman said that Lee Michael John had progressed enough to enter another sphere and that she would be taking him herself. It was explained to Debbie that her dreams were not really ordinary dreams at all but what she was experiencing was astral projection and that in fact she had entered the spirit world while her physical body was asleep.

Debbie was told that she would not see her son again until she passed over into the spirit realms, but her grandmother promised to love the child and teach him all the things that Debbie would have done. Debbie says, 'I nodded and tearfully passed Lee Michael John back to Grandmother. I smothered him with kisses and then Grandmother led him back towards the bridge. I waved to them and they walked over the bridge and out of sight. Strangely enough, I was not tempted to go after them. The next thing I knew I was awake.'

Debbie feels as she looks back on the experience that she is part of some strange plan. She says, 'Lee wasn't like an earth child. He seemed angelic.'

Since the dreams, which have now stopped, Debbie has become pregnant again and is looking forward to the birth of her new baby. She says, 'I feel that everything that has happened has been carefully worked out for my well-being. I am glad I had astral projection and have been greatly comforted by it and I know that there is life after death, and that my son is being well looked after. I only wish that more people could experience such a wonderful thing.'

Mrs Barbara Hoole, a kindly grandmother from Cheltenham was devastated when the joy of her life, her beautiful grandchild Siobhan, died of a cot death at the age of eight months.

Mrs Hoole remembers the horror of the moment when she realized that the baby had died. She says, 'She was put down as usual for her afternoon rest, a happy, seemingly healthy, normal baby, but when her mother went to the cot later and picked her up, the baby just flopped over her arm like a rag doll, for she was dead.'

There was a very special rapport between Mrs Hoole and Siobhan and just previously, the old lady had been seriously ill in hospital. She recalls, 'The family would bring the baby in to see me and put her into my arms. She would gaze at me fixedly, tiny though she was. It was as if she was trying to give me a message. I got the clear impression that she was trying to tell me that I wasn't going to die, as everyone, including the doctors, thought, but that I was going to get better. She was right, bless her. I did get better. If only I could have gone instead of her.'

'After the baby died, I had a strange recurring dream,' says Mrs Hoole. 'The baby used to come to me as a little barefoot child wearing a floating, short, blue shift. Her hair was short and fluffy and she had such a happy laughing face as she stretched her hands out to me.'

Mrs Hoole feels that the baby is trying to show her that death is not the end. She says, 'The strangest thing is that before the dreams started, I always imagined the child as I last saw her, a small bouncy baby, but each time she appears to me in my dream she is slightly different, as if she is slowly growing up. She is no longer a baby. She died in April, 1980, and it seems that she has since then developed into a toddler and is able to walk, just like a normal two-year-old girl would.'

The above cases have one thing in common, although the circumstances are different, and that is that each one suggests not only that life continues after death, but that there are great efforts being made to bring to us the proof of this fact by various methods: materialization, astral travel or dreams.

Part Two

Hypnotic Regression

There are many accounts of people who under hypnosis have been regressed to various stages in their lives; in some instances back to the womb and beyond. Often very colourful and dramatic past lives are tapped and events are described in great detail.

In countless cases valuable hypnotherapy can be carried out to help people solve a particular problem such as alcoholism, gambling, smoking, compulsive eating, kleptomania, etc., and even physical illnesses can be cured by using regressive hypnotism to pin-point the origin of the illness, and then forcing the patient to face up to the conditions which originally caused the illness, thus coming to terms with those conditions, leading to a cure or disappearance of the symptoms.

There is no doubt that hypnotherapy plays a useful role in our society today, but this must not be confused with the other type of hypnotic regression which is not concerned with any medical or sociological problems and is performed solely for the purpose of regressing a hypnotized subject back to a real or imagined previous life.

In extremely rare cases, the subject may possibly be retrieving memories of past lives, but the hard evidence for this is almost non-existent. In almost every case investigated there arises at some point a serious insurmountable obstacle to the validity of the claimed previous life.

For example, a man may, under hypnosis, give an elaborate description of life as a Roman centurion with an impressive wealth of detail, but instead of this being the manifestation of a previous life, it could be nothing more than the surfacing of data which had previously been fed through to his brain from long-forgotten experiences in his present life, via a book, a film, a newspaper article, etc. Although this information would be completely forgotten by his conscious mind, it would, nevertheless, be stored in his brain and could be recalled at any time by the hypnotic technique.

In this age of mass communication there are endless opportunities for picking up knowledge, and considering that every single experience, feeling and thought which has ever occurred to us is lodged in our brains, it is not surprising that many long-forgotten experiences can be drawn into the area of consciousness in a misleading manner. Because these experiences appear to be totally new to the conscious mind, they can often give the impression of being incidents from another life.

One very well-known and respected hypnotist who practises regression sums it up by saying, 'If I could have found it out so could my client.' He means, of course, that if evidence exists to verify that a certain incident has occurred in the past, then the very fact that this evidence does exist and can be researched makes it possible, however improbable, that the evidence had, one way or another, consciously or subconsciously, reached the client's brain, and lay there computerized and ready to spring to the fore at the appropriate time, i.e. when the client was under the hypnotic influence. On the other hand, if there is no evidence available to substantiate the subject's story, then how can it be proved at all?

The main question to consider is the order in which the experience and the verification registered in the brain of the client or subject. The answer to this question is the crucial pointer as to whether or not the subject is really remembering a previous existence or merely recalling past incidents from his present life.

Unfortunately the question is not easily answered, due to the fact that we are dealing with subconscious experiences. If, as in extremely isolated cases, the experience or mind picture registered before the subject had any knowledge of a particular incident, either conscious or subconscious, then there is a strong indication that the subject did indeed experience such an incident at some point in his existence and that the experience is lodged in the memory of the subject.

We must also consider the possibility that a subject, knowing that he was to be hypnotized, and not wishing to let the hypnotist down, as it were, invented a plausible story, either deliberately or not. There are many examples in which the subject pre-conditions himself by auto-suggestion or a type of self-hypnosis so that when he is then put into the trance by the hypnotist, he is certain to come up with the appropriate response.

The power of suggestion must not be underestimated. There are many instances of people behaving in a totally illogical manner simply because they have been led to believe that this is how they should react.

For example, an experiment was set up where four people known to suffer from hay fever were subjected to the following test. They were blindfolded and told that a small bowl of pollen was being placed under their chins. They were then asked to dip their fingers into the bowl to feel the pollen dust. The subjects did this, but unknown to them, instead of pollen dust they were in fact dipping their fingers into bowls of cornflour. They were then asked to breathe in over the pollen dust. In every case, the breathing produced all the symptoms of hay fever – sneezing, irritation of the eyes and nose, etc. After a little time elapsed, the same four subjects were lined up, again blindfolded, and this time they were told that they would be breathing from bowls of cornflour – in fact, bowls filled with pollen. The result was that although each of the four subjects was a known hay fever sufferer, not one single person reacted to the pollen when they had been pre-conditioned to believe that they were only breathing cornflour.

In the same way, if there is a suggestion, either stated verbally or simply inferred, there is a strong tendency in most subjects to comply with that suggestion, so when a session is set up with a hypnotist with a view to regressing the subject to a previous life, then because the subject may well feel compelled to give the desired and expected results, he will relate all kinds of weird and wonderful experiences. This does not indicate that the subject is being consciously deceitful in any way, it is merely that he has reacted to the suggestion.

It is interesting to note that in stage hypnotism, the subjects are carefully selected by the hypnotist. This may not be made apparent to the audience, especially if he is a skilled showman, but nevertheless he will only work with subjects whom he knows for sure will be responsive to his suggestions.

As far as the audience is concerned, they see a random group of people rush up on to the stage in answer to the hypnotist's request for volunteers. They are indeed exactly what they appear to be – just ordinary members of the public. But once they are on the stage the hypnotist goes into a carefully-planned process of elimination which is presented in such a way as to make the audience think that it is all part of the main act, when in fact it is only a precautionary preliminary to the main event.

Usually the elimination routine will go as follows: The group of people on the stage will be asked to carry out a simple instruction, such as having to clasp their hands over their heads. The hypnotist will then say that on the count of three the volunteers will find it impossible to unclasp their hands. He will then watch closely to see which of the volunteers immediately unclasp their hands and which of them comply with his suggestion and remain with their hands tightly clasped together. At this stage he will recognize any extroverts amongst the volunteers as they will already be putting on a great show of straining and grimacing to give the impression that they are trying desperately to separate their hands.

From this simple demonstration, the hypnotist can spot the best subjects. He will ask the people who unclasped their hands straight away to leave the stage, usually to a round of applause. He may then do a follow-up experiment with the remaining volunteers in order to classify them into further susceptibility categories. While this is being done, the hypnotist will keep up a constant line of patter so that his audience is not aware of the fact that he is still evaluating his subjects.

The stage hypnotist will soon select in his mind his star performers and he will then choose one of these and with the confidence that the subject can't wait to take the spotlight, he will carry out some spectacular trick which will cause the audience to roar with laughter or gasp in awe.

Most of these hypnotic stunts are nothing more than optical illusions – tricks of the trade – whereby a relatively simple feat is trumped up and presented as if it was something incredibly difficult which can only be performed because the subject has been put into a so-called deep hypnotic trance. Normally, the clever showman will try to impress his audience with high-falutin' phraseology, thus lending himself a stamp of authority and credibility.

Perhaps there is something of the showman in all of us, and under hypnosis we are provided with a shield to hide behind in order to protect our true personality and identity, and forget about our inhibitions.

This tendency to perform in a certain way to overshadow deep-seated problems can lead to a variety of complex phobias and psychological conditions. It is in this area that hypnotherapy is especially valuable. One practising hypnotherapist attached to the Institute of Biodynamic Therapy in London had a telephone call from the doctor of a patient who had all the outward symptoms of heart trouble, yet even after extensive tests, and visits to a Harley Street consultant, there was no sign of any malfunctioning of the heart. The patient was an attractive middle-aged woman who had been happily married for twelve years to the same man. She regularly complained of pains across her chest and forearms, and she had what she described as palpitations and heart rhythm problems.

The hypnotherapist relaxed the woman and put her into a trance. He asked her to go back to the first time that she experienced the heart trouble. The woman was able to recall vividly that she had been having dinner with her husband and in the course of general conversation he remarked that he hoped that she had had a nice day, and then he asked her what she had done that afternoon. The woman instantly suffered a heart attack, or what appeared to be a heart attack.

Delving deeper into the matter, the hypnotist then asked the woman to go back to earlier on that afternoon and to tell him what she had been doing. The woman described how she had gone out shopping that afternoon and by chance she happened to meet an old boyfriend, someone she had been very attracted to before she met and married her husband. She only spoke to her ex-flame for a few minutes but with continual encouragement from the hypnotist, the woman admitted that while she was talking to this old friend she started to feel strongly attracted to him. In her mind she had tried to fight against this attraction because it made her feel uneasy and she felt guilty because of her attraction to a man other than her husband.

Later on that evening when the woman's husband asked her what she had done that afternoon, all her feelings of guilt came to the fore, confusing her so much that her only way out was to simulate a heart attack. The tactic worked because the husband got such a shock that he dropped the line of questioning immediately.

Once the trend had been set, the woman was forced to maintain her line of defence by continuing to have these attacks, which were so subtly contrived by her own subconscious efforts that even the woman herself did not know how or why she was having the attacks.

When the hypnotist brought the woman face to face with the underlying motive behind her heart attacks, she was able to come to terms with the whole thing, and of course the attacks ceased.

It remains true that many people have been regressed under hypnosis into what they sincerely believe to be their previous lives. David Stevenson, Senior Lecturer in International Community Health at the Liverpool School of Tropical Medicine, who has worked in Africa as a mission doctor and for the Malawi Government, wrote the foreword to Monica O'Hara's book, *New Hope Through Hypnotherapy*, in which he states, 'Regression into the memories of previous personalities can also sometimes cure anxieties and disabilities in this life. Fear of water or of heights may be traced to a memory of drowning or falling. Realization that a nightmare or a phobia is due to something past and done with, rather than something likely to happen in the future, can dispel fear.

'Though modern science may tend to dismiss such phenomena as superstition, or ignore them as being inconvenient to the usual scientific picture of the Universe, careful recording of the phenomena and investigation of those memories which can be checked for historical or other accuracy is in fact scientific research. If a sufficient body of this is built up then science will have to accept it and fit it into the normal pattern of belief, much as once upon a time the Establishment had to accept that the World is round and not flat!

'Science and the Church may find that they have much in common, both in restricting acknowledgement of these phenomena and in the need to accept and adapt to their existence once acknowledgement can no longer be denied. Some scientists and churchmen do, of course, already accept that they do exist and that they should be more fully investigated and understood.

'Modification of the materialism of much of our present society and of the short-term views of our politicians might be a useful effect of better understanding. It may be we, ourselves, who shall have to live with the environmental desolation and radioactive waste which we may leave to our grandchildren if we are not careful. That might serve us right, but realization of the possibility could help us to avoid it. In some African societies a new-born child may be referred to as "Grandfather" in the belief that he is indeed his grandfather reborn.

'If we have lived (and died) before, there is less need to fear, or desperately try to postpone, dying again. A greater willingness to talk about death seems helpful to those who have fatal illnesses and to their families and friends.

'It is an irony of our society in these islands that we are now too humanitarian to execute a known murderer but are content to terminate the lives of over 100,000 unborn children a year through abortion. What is the correct balance between the slogans to be seen on walls in Liverpool: "A Woman's Right to Choose" and "A Child's Right to Life"? One might argue that if reincarnation occurs, then abortion, to end an inconvenient pregnancy, merely postpones that individual's return to Earth. But those who support easy abortion tend to do so in the belief that the unborn child's mind is a blank slate on which nothing has yet been written. If it is a being with memories of earlier lives, or with an immortal soul, then that changes the situation.'

In a letter published in the *British Medical Association News Review*, headed *Foetal Memories*, Dr Stevenson writes, 'I have sat in on a great many sessions of hypnotic regression with the Liverpool hypnotherapist Joe Keeton in which he has taken people back, under hypnosis, to memories of times before they were born. Many of these people produce vivid and convincing memories of previous personalities . . .

'Some people are totally unwilling to accept these memories as anything other than fantasy. Others take them as evidence for reincarnation. I have tried to trace three doctors, mentioned in these memories, in the Medical Registers in the B.M.A. Library, but have found no trace of them – though I found without difficulty my father and his uncle who were medical practitioners at about the same date as given in the memories.

'It may be very difficult to decide whether an adult, under hypnosis, is producing genuine memories or a mixture of memories and fantasies based on forgotten experiences, reading and radio and television programmes, absorbed between childhood and adulthood. Clearer evidence of memory of previous personalities can be found in examining the cases of young children, too young to have done any reading, and often in communities where there is not yet television who produce, soon after they learn to talk, accounts of previous lives as identifiable individuals, usually living near, in both time and space, to their present homes.

'We should not refuse to examine such evidence just because, if memories of previous lives can be demonstrated, the implications for our present systems of belief and action may be considerable. If facts can be demonstrated then we have to adapt to them.'

While hypnotism serves its purpose, and may be one possible method of retrieving memory of previous lives, it is, by its very nature, fraught with doubts, ifs and buts. Also the majority of subjects regressed through hypnotism are adults with a lifetime's store of knowledge and experience to draw upon, thereby supplying sufficient raw material for the reconstruction of a supposed previous life.

Hypnotism has played no part in any of the case histories covered in this book. In each and every case, the child has given spontaneous information of their memories of their previous lives. Without exception, the initial statements of the children have come completely out of the blue without any related foregoing conversation whatever.

Part Three

Medical and Religious Views

Medical Views

The main aim of members of the medical profession is to enhance the quality of life on earth by caring for the physical body. One eminent London consultant remembers the advice given to him by his mentor in his student days: 'Just make sure the body is free from the danger of infection and then leave it alone to get on with the work of healing itself.'

There is no denying that a good night's sleep goes a long way towards curing many of our minor ailments. What happens during this period of sleep which causes us to wake up feeling refreshed and cured? What forces have been at work while our bodies have been asleep? Something must have happened to alleviate the aches and pains and discomfort which affected us on retiring the previous night.

One possible explanation could be that the revitalizing repair-work was done by the etheric body, which is the non-material counterpart of the physical body. During sleep, the consciousness blanks out, thus allowing the body to relax completely. Then the etheric body takes over and recharges the flow of vital energy into the cells affected, causing them to make a speedy recovery.

Many people would argue that the cells of the body do this repair-work by themselves. It is a proven fact that the body cells are continually dying and being discarded, and are replaced by new cells which have been forming meanwhile. The question is, what makes this happen? What form of energy activates the birth of a new cell?

Let us look upon the physical body as a type of computer which has been programmed to operate under certain conditions, i.e. when the previously established number of cells are working with perfect efficiency. When a cell withers away and dies due to various causes such as the effects of sun, wind, injury, etc., a new cell automatically replaces the dead cell, as dictated by the programme. This replacement process, however, must be carried out by the exercise of some type of energy, and some directing force must spark off the whole procedure.

If we can accept the idea that a human being is made up of more than just the material body, then many questions can be answered. The etheric, or non-physical, body could be the linking influence between various reincarnations.

Each time a soul becomes incarnate in the flesh, the physical body will be different because it is formed from different parents, but the etheric body, containing the soul, spirit and essence of the personality, remains the same, and it is within this etheric body that impressions affecting us, during reincarnations on earth, are lodged. The etheric body then passes on these impressions to the physical consciousness, thus giving flashes of scenes and incidents from a previous existence.

This transparent etheric body which permeates the physical contains all the impressions of previous incarnations including a replica of all injuries and damage to previous physical bodies. Some babies are born with evidence of these previous injuries in the form of scars, birthmarks and deformities, as in the case of young Dominic who was born a healthy beautiful baby with a scar on the front of his right thigh. It looks exactly like a stab scar – a raised white line of flesh which remains white when the rest of his body gets tanned. Just before the child's third birthday he was standing up on a chair to look at a picture on the wall, and his grandmother who was standing by the chair gently touched the scar, which had never been referred to before. Dominic astonished his grandmother and his mother by saying, 'Man on boat did that with big knife. Lots of blood everywhere, all covered in blood.' When his mother asked him what happened after that, he said, 'Fell in water and got drowned.' The child then looked as if he was going to cry, but he went on to say that his name had been Olaf and that his sister had been called Zita. When his mother asked him if he knew Zita now, Dominic replied, 'Yes, she's you, Mummy.'

Dominic has always been terrified of water, and he used to cry so much when his mother was bathing him that she was forced to give it up as a bad job and just sponge him down instead. The scar is still to be seen on the boy's leg and it grows with him.

His mother confirms that Dominic has never ever been on a boat of any description, and that he certainly has never been confronted by a man brandishing a knife. His mother was surprised at the remarks about blood because he had never seen blood before and she didn't think he even knew what blood meant.

It is the non-physical body which continues to exist after death, independent of the physical body which is really only an outer shell which decays as soon as it is separated from the etheric, at death. The etheric body then goes on to exist on a different plane of vibration. These vibrations can be likened to energy waves, but as yet science has not succeeded in locating them. However this need hardly mean that they do not exist. Before radio waves were discovered people would never have believed such a thing was possible; nevertheless the waves were all around us just waiting on someone to declare their existence. The time will surely come when these vibrations will be known to all of us and perhaps then they will become accepted as part of our lives, or more accurately, as part of our after-lives. This would undoubtedly dispel the fear of death which to some people makes living intolerable.

Often inherited memory – or, as it is sometimes referred to, genetic memory – is put forward as an explanation for cases claiming reincarnation.

As an example of how this would work, let us look at the Mandy case history. Mandy's mother was present at the funeral of the first baby who died at the age of five months. The distressed mother almost fell into the grave. This traumatic experience would be strongly imprinted in her mind. When she gave birth to Mandy Number Two her genes were passed on to the new baby influencing the child's physical attributes and tendencies. Could it be possible that the mother's memories and experiences were also passed on to the child via the genes, thus implanting the impressions received by the mother at the graveside incident?

Genetic memory can no doubt play some part in explaining odd behaviour in children, but because it cannot possibly account for all the aspects of the Mandy case, it would be unwise to rely on this as the explanation. It is true that although the silver bracelet was buried with the baby, her mother saw this bracelet and knew that it had been buried in the coffin. That impression could have been transferred from the mother to Mandy Number Two, but what about the yellow fluffy ball? Mandy Number Two remembers this being buried with her, a fact of which her mother was totally unaware. How could a memory be passed on to a child by a parent who never experienced it in the first place?

Another important factor regarding the Mandy case is that any possible genetic influence could only have come from one of her parents, her mother, because the father of the first Mandy was not the father of the second Mandy. Also there are the remarks about Stephen to take into consideration. Here, there is no blood link whatever between the first Mandy and Stephen, but there is a 50% connection between the second Mandy and Stephen, both having the same father. Could the second Mandy's remarks about Stephen come about by either genetic influence, or by some form of telepathy from father to daughter? This may be a possibility, but the words 'He can walk now' would make one question this suggestion. George Seabrook remembered his son as a cripple in a wheelchair who had never been able to walk. The only other explanation could be that deep down in Mr Seabrook's subconscious he was telling himself that his son could walk now, and these thoughts had been telepathically picked up by Mandy.

Dr Peter Fenwick, Neurophysiologist at St Thomas's

Hospital, London and Senior Lecturer at the Institute of Psychiatry, feels that in Mandy's case it would be unlikely that inherited memory is the explanation. In his view, it is much more logical to suggest that she heard these or similar statements from the mother and was repeating them. It is, however, a logical possibility that reincarnation is the answer. Dr Fenwick feels that genetic memory is probably ruled out when we remember Mandy's words, 'Why did you cry when I died? Didn't you know I would come back?' Dr Fenwick says, 'This is a very telling statement because it is unlikely to have come from the mother.'

It is significant that most of the cases which come to light are toddlers between the ages of two and three. Could it be that most people are born with certain memories of previous existence imprinted in their minds, and as soon as they can make themselves understood they start to describe people, places, incidents and experiences of their past lives. The majority of parents just fob their children off, thinking that the stories are childish gibberish inspired by vivid imagination, and the stories die a natural death. Possibly by the time speech becomes coherent all memories of life before birth have already faded. In almost every case, by the time the children reach school age all talk of previous life ceases. It could be that because of the increasing demands made upon the child, these pre-birth memories are pushed to the back of the mind and into the subconscious. This would explain the ever-increasing number of cases in which the subconscious reveals a wealth of facts appertaining to previous existence through hypnotic regression. The facts could hardly be revealed if they were not there in the first place.

Dr Fenwick mentioned scientific work which shows that the brain rhythms of babies in the last month before birth show changes which have been interpreted as periods during which they may be dreaming.

This strongly suggests that the unborn child experiences dreams. We may well ask what the baby could be dreaming about, since it has not as yet had any of the experiences of life upon which earthly dreams are founded. Could the unborn baby possibly be dreaming about a previous life in another realm?

Recent evidence shows that the foetus can hear, feel and see in the womb, and this ties in with the many accounts of young children remembering their impressions during their foetal days. Some were aware of extreme darkness, others of golden light; most got the feeling of being wet; and almost all of the reports confirm that being an unborn baby is indeed a noisy business. All kinds of descriptions of noise have been put forward by small children trying to describe what they heard before they were born: splashing, chug-chug, loud talking, and just plain noisy.

The sound factor is one of the most important in connection with the baby's emotional development. Ordinary everyday sounds can filter through to the womb whether it's the shrill ringing of an alarm clock, the sound of a jet plane screaming overhead, or the sounds of conversation. It is interesting to note that in Japan, pregnant women are banned from working in noisy factories because of the risk that the foetus could be adversely affected, and might, in later life, suffer from psychosomatic problems.

The differences reported in connection with what the children remember seeing whilst in the womb could be accounted for by the fact that the foetus does sleep, so during sleep (excluding R.E.M. sleep) they could have experienced the blackness, and during waking moments they could have been aware of light, either golden or just of comparative brightness.

Dr Arthur Guirdham, a psychiatrist from Bath, well known for his work with children suffering from nightmares, is convinced that in many cases, the bad dreams are due to traumatic experiences in previous lives. This explanation can very often account for phobias and odd behaviour in children where the parents cannot trace any significant incident that could possibly be responsible. In many cases, neurotic behaviour was traced back to a previous violent death, such as a stabbing, drowning, railway accident, etc. These children show a morbid fear of knives, water, trains and so on.

Dr Guirdham also feels that difficult labours can lead to obsessional conditions in adult life – phobias, anxiety, etc. – and he states 'The foetus/child becomes aware of duration too early due to the uterine inertia associated with difficult births.'

The mother's emotional state during pregnancy has far-reaching effects on the baby, especially during the first three months. That is the crucial time when all the organs are formed and when the child is most at risk from drugs, alcohol and especially nicotine, which is detrimental to the child's normal progress within the womb.

An unborn child can interpret maternal depression and stress, and reacts to this. When a person becomes depressed, every single cell in the body is part of that depression, and therefore the negative feelings are communicated to the baby who in turn suffers along with the mother.

If the pregnant mother allows herself to fall into a pessimistic frame of mind there is a very real danger that her attitude could start off a chain of events which could lead to actual physical illness. It is a known fact that too much dwelling on sad or morbid thoughts can lead to gall-bladder trouble and liver ailments, which do nothing for the physical or emotional condition of the mother-to-be.

We are what we think, and if we insist on taking a depressive, negative attitude, for whatever reasons, imagined or otherwise, and swamping ourselves in thoughts of misery, we could start off an irreversible process effecting the organs and glands of the body thus preventing normal activity, the outcome of which could range from loss of appetite, lethargy, inability to concentrate or think clearly, immobility, leading to a variety of conditions including severe malnutrition, insanity, coma and even death.

We can see where constant depressive thoughts can lead us, but the opposite is also true. If we think happy thoughts these in turn effect our outlook on life and we begin to see that things are not all bad. Even the darkest tunnel has light at the end of it, although sometimes it cannot be perceived at first glance. Everyone on earth has troubles. How we handle them is dependent upon one thing: attitude of mind.

Therefore, when the foetus is subjected to pleasant and calming influences the baby will respond positively. This fact is substantiated by evidence accumulated by Dr Michele Clements of the City of London Maternity Hospital, who with the help of Yehudi Menuhin, the world-famous violinist, some time ago tested a number of ante-natal patients to see if their unborn babies would respond to music. The babies showed interesting reactions which pointed to the fact that the majority of them favoured the flute and violin above the other instruments used in the experiment.

Nowadays most mothers-to-be are familiar with ultra-sound scan equipment used to monitor the movements of the foetus on a television screen making it possible to chart the development of the baby. By measuring the head, the expected date of delivery can be verified. If there are any abnormalities discovered, more detailed tests can be carried out whereby some of the fluid surrounding the foetus is drawn off, then analysed by examining the chromosomes to locate conditions such as Downs Syndrome (Mongolism).

This brings us on to the difficult question of abortion, and all the related medical and moral principles. The main moral consideration when dealing with the subject of abortion surely must be to establish the moment when the soul, spirit, life-force, call it what you will, becomes united with the physical foetus. If, as our evidence in the case histories suggests, this life-force and the consciousness which contains the personality, is present not only in the womb, but also before conception, then there is every possibility that it could also be present throughout the entire nine months of pregnancy. Remember, a lifeless foetus can hardly have dreams, yet dream-pattern E.E.G. readings have been recorded in unborn babies.

If this possibility exists, however slight, then perhaps we would do well to review the current law and attitudes regarding abortion.

The laws of life operate in mysterious ways, and we can't hope to understand all of them. Since the regular use of ultra-sound equipment in ante-natal clinics, a most inexplicable phenomenon has puzzled doctors and patients alike. It is the case of the dreaded vanishing foetus whereby a mother diagnosed by her scan results as expecting twins, goes back for a further scan only to find to her horror that one of her babies has disappeared without trace.

Dr H. P. Robinson, obstetrician and gynaecologist at the Queen Mother's Hospital, Department of Midwifery, Glasgow University, has been carrying out extensive tests to try to solve the mystery.

One possible explanation is that the tissue of the baby is completely absorbed into the body of the mother. After all, the tissue of a foetus is not that foreign to the mother, so there would not necessarily be any systemic problems such as poisoning, and the other foetus apparently is not physically affected. Whether or not the remaining twin suffers emotionally in later life due to the sudden disappearance of its womb companion is another matter, and in fact one case history shows that a surviving twin grieved throughout childhood for the twin who didn't make it through to birth.

The most distressing cases of vanishing foetus occur when ultra-sound tests have not been carried out throughout the pregnancy. A mother could be happy in the knowledge that she has been indisputably diagnosed as bearing twins. As it draws near to her confinement she excitedly makes her preparations for the birth of her two babies, providing two of everything, and she prepares herself psychologically for the great event.

When delivery day arrives, and only one baby is born with no sign of the other twin, the mother is totally devastated. She cannot understand what has happened because if her second twin was not born dead, where could it be? At this stage, when all the post-natal problems are setting in, the mother could start to harbour all kinds of delusions about her missing baby. Who took it? Why? In such circumstances the mother usually takes a long time to adjust herself emotionally.

As in cases of natural abortion, the vanishing foetus is another example of nature's great plan. For some reason the second twin is not meant to be born. We can assume that the souls of these children return whence they came to await the correct moment for them to be born again on earth.

When a fluke of nature occurs, such as the vanishing foetus, still birth, etc., perhaps it may be explained by taking into consideration the ever-changing circumstances of the world and everyone in it. Say, for example, that a certain child is due to be born to certain parents, and during the pregnancy, either consciously or subconsciously, the mother has a change of attitude towards the baby which leads to the mother secretly wishing that she did not have to bear the child, then it may be a logical conclusion drawn by Divine Providence that the child would not benefit from being born to that particular mother.

Religious Views

The Protestant church, including Anglican, Presbyterian, Methodist, Baptist, United Reform, Church of Scotland, Pentecostal, Lutheran, Welsh Congregational, Adventist and others, does not generally accept reincarnation. From Lambeth Palace, headquarters of the Church of England, a spokesman for the Archbishop of Canterbury states, 'This is not a subject on which there are any official Christian views. As you are probably aware, a very long time ago the Church threw out any idea of reincarnation. No evidence has since been forthcoming to suggest any reconsideration. If there was forthcoming evidence I have no doubt that it would be considered, but at the moment what evidence there is must be left in the category at least of "not proven".'

The Roman Catholic Church does not accept reincarnation because this is not seen as part of God's revelation. Life on Earth is looked upon as a period of decision and choice whereby we choose to follow a life of good or evil. We die once and according to the state of our immortal soul at the time of death, and taking into consideration the choices and decisions taken throughout the lifetime, it goes on to Heaven, Purgatory or Hell. Heaven is to enter the sight of God; Purgatory is a place of purification for souls who die in union with God but still require further preparation before reaching a state worthy of entering Heaven; Hell is the resting place for souls who, during their lives on Earth, have cut themselves off from God. It was stated that although it is accepted that Hell exists it is not known if anyone is there or not.

The Church of Christ, Scientist, states that reincarnation has no part in its teaching, although it does believe that in death the spirit continues to exist in a state which is determined by the type of life which was led on earth.

Some Christian Spiritualists accept reincarnation and some do not, although the majority believe that it can and does occur. Their main objective is to prove to the world that life continues after physical death and they hold demonstrations of clairvoyance in most spiritualist churches whereby a medium gives messages from departed people to their relatives, relating personal data which could not be known by the medium, thereby providing evidence that the dead person really still exists and can communicate. They believe that all of us have spirit guides who help us in our everyday lives and who act as go-betweens in contacting deceased relatives and friends.

Mormons do not accept reincarnation but they do believe in life before birth in the form of a pre-mortal spirit existence. They state, 'These spirit beings, the offspring of exalted parents, men and women, appearing in all respects as mortal persons do, excepting only that their spirit bodies are made of a more pure and refined substance than the elements from which mortal bodies are made.'

It is a Mormon belief that since one of the purposes of earthly life is that we should live by faith, the memory of this pre-Earth life with the Heavenly Father is generally blotted out. Life is eternal, the spirit of man never dies and the universal re-uniting of spirit and body is promised to all. At physical death, to each of us will come the rewards and punishments earned on earth with eternal progression and happiness the ultimate hope of all.

The Greek Orthodox Church does not accept reincarnation and is of the belief that when a person dies they go to either Heaven or Hell. This is a once only and final destiny. It states that if a soul is damned to Hell then there is no escape from that doom. It terms Hell as a state in which the soul is forced to be turned away from God. Heaven on the other hand is a state whereby the soul is united with God whom in Greek Orthodoxy is called Theos. Whatever has been achieved on earth dictates the route which the soul will take at physical death. Once a person dies that person cannot do anything to help himself but the prayers of people still alive on earth can help the soul of the dead person to progress.

Jehovah's Witnesses do not accept reincarnation but they believe that after death everyone will rise at the final resurrection to be judged, according to the type of life each person has led on earth. This rising up of the dead reunites the departed spirit with the revitalized physical body. Therefore every person will come back as the person they were originally and not as the same spirit clothed in a different physical body, which is of course the accepted idea of reincarnation.

The New Church was founded on the teachings of Emanuel Swedenborg who was born in Sweden in 1688, and died in 1772. It does not support reincarnation, mainly because of the belief that it is not necessary to live more than one life on Earth in order to prepare for eternal life. Life is believed to continue after death in what is termed the world of spirits, in which the soul continues its life prior to its final destiny in either Heaven or Hell. The purpose of life in the material world is that the ruling love of a man may be established. Once this is formed for good or evil, then the state of life after death is a state of preparation.

Swedenborg believed that there are with all men, spirits from the unseen world in close association. The spirits who are with us have themselves lived on Earth when they were in the body. An explanation of reincarnation is given as the result of these companion spirits communicating from their own memories with the minds of the people they are watching over on Earth. In this way, a man will have a recollection of something he has never seen or heard, and he will attribute this to his own personal memory of previous existence.

Buddhists do not accept reincarnation as such, but they

do believe in re-birth on earth which to them is something different, involving a process of mind and body interacting throughout the cosmos. In Buddhism there is no God, no soul, no spirit, only living beings concerned with the enlightenment of mind and body, achieved by following the middle way – the path of perfect balance.

Buddhists believe that the body fuels the mind in as much as it provides the energy upon which the force of the mind feeds, and although the mind is dependent upon the physical body for its vital energy, the charged mind then takes over the role of controller of the material body. However they also believe that the mind can exist without a body.

Buddha did not accept that death brought eternal happiness to some and eternal misery for others. He taught that life and death follow on from one another so that any particular lifetime on earth will be subjected to conditions laid down by ourselves in past lives based on the degree of moral development we attained in that past life, i.e. if a person speaks or acts with an evil mind, unhappiness will follow him, and if a person speaks or acts with a pure mind, happiness will follow him. The body ages, dies and deteriorates but the mind survives death. All things that come into being are the effect of causes and conditions, which themselves act as causes and conditions in turn again, to give rise to other effects, and so it goes on.

The Islamic belief does not include the acceptance of reincarnation. There is only one life on earth and at death the soul is separated from the body and goes on to Heaven or Hell.

Hell is looked upon as a kind of hospital where the soul is treated in order to make it worthy to enter the realms of Heaven. This recuperation period in Hell is fortunately always an intermediary stage and is never under any circumstances an eternal fate or punishment, because God, known as Allah, is all merciful.

In Heaven, and in Hell, the soul is given ample

opportunity for learning and advancement and according to how these are embraced and dealt with, the soul gradually progresses in an upward direction towards God, or Allah. If the soul rejects the opportunity for advancement then it stays static in its Hellish plane of existence until such time as there is a change of attitude. Every action and decision is motivated by the free will of the soul.

The Hindu religion, in marked contrast to all the rest, is entirely based upon the concept of reincarnation, according to Karma – the record of good and evil accumulated during life on earth. Every person comes back to the earth many many times in order to balance their Karma, i.e. work off any outstanding debts owed by the soul. The circumstances into which a person may be born are determined by the condition of that person's Karma before birth. If the person, in a previous life on earth, had been, say, extremely short-tempered and impatient, the balance of that soul could be restored by means of a rebirth on earth into circumstances whereby that soul will learn to be more patient. This could be achieved in various ways – perhaps that person will be destined to choose a wife who is a patient loving person, and from her example the person will learn patience himself.

However, things may not always work out in such an amicable way. It could be that for the guaranteed advancement of the soul, and to ensure that the person really does learn patience, he might be taught the hard way. For example he may be born into a family in which some member is severely handicapped; thus the person will be compelled to exercise patience. Another possibility would be that the person could father a child who turns out to possess the same impatient traits that the person himself displayed in his previous life. By having to deal with such a child, it would become apparent to the father that patience is indeed a virtue.

So in this way, by operating the law of Karma, all misdeeds are atoned for, all unfinished works are completed, all evil thoughts and actions are wiped out by a corresponding good thought and action. The Karma of a person stays with them throughout the continual cycle of births and deaths and is a permanent part of the consciousness or soul. It usually takes many incarnations in the flesh to work off all of our Karmic debts, but when this is completed, and the perfect balance of the soul is attained, then there is no need for further reincarnations and the soul has reached the ultimate state of perfection and immortality known as Nirvana.

When a man and woman conceive a child, the type of child which will be born to them will depend upon various factors, that is the Karma of the mother, the father and the child. If, resulting from the Karma built up from their previous lives, the mother and the father are destined to have a saintly child born to them, then when a saintly child is ready to be born, that child will be sent to those particular parents. It can sometimes happen that, again according to an individual's Karmic content, he is re-born as a lion; and a cow could be born as a person. According to the Hindu philosophy the law of Karma applies to every facet of existence, human or not.

Scientologists do accept reincarnation, and believe that what we sow in one life, we reap in another. There is an emphasis on continually trying to improve the spiritual side of life which they believe lives on as an independent force when the physical body dies.

They believe that over the years there has been a steady decline of moral values which has resulted in the formation of certain attitudes, i.e. a leaning towards the materialistic side of life as opposed to the more spiritual outlook. They are concerned with the great increase in neurotic and psychic diseases and they try to offer practical help in this direction by counselling and, when necessary, regression.

Jews believe that when they die their souls go to God via Purgatory where they stay for a time of reflection and possible retribution. Jewish opinions are divided on the question of reincarnation, although their mystic tradition affirmed the doctrine of the transmigration of souls and this was accepted by the Rabbis.

According to Jewish beliefs there is a complete scheme of reward and punishment which can be observed in operation. Louis Jacobs gives an example of this in his book, *A Jewish Theology*. He states it is the view of the Jewish Kabbalists, 'If good men suffer in a national catastrophe this is because once the decree has gone forth it must embrace all without exception, unless it be that of the man so righteous that he deserves to be saved. But one who is partly to blame, i.e. because he failed to rebuke the others for their misdeeds will perish with them. It is also true that an especially great saint may have the power to save even the wicked. A wicked man may be blessed with prosperity in order that he might serve as an instrument for the fulfilment of God's purpose. He may, for example have a righteous son who will inherit his wealth and use it for good purposes. When a woman miscarries this is because of her own sins and also because the embryo deserves the punishment because of the sins he had committed in a previous existence. This explains too, why innocent children suffer. They are not, in fact, innocent but are guilty of sins committed in a previous incarnation.'

In the same publication Louis Jacobs states, 'What can a modern Jew believe on this whole question of the Hereafter? It depends on which type of modern Jew we mean. Some modern Jews clearly have no use for any doctrine of a Hereafter and, oddly enough, this includes some religious Jews. But it is surely a very curious religious outlook which limits man's opportunities for encountering God to the brief span of this life . . . Can it be believed that God has created only to destroy, that all man's hopes and dreams of a higher life are doomed to frustration? Nor is it much use speaking of individuals living on in their children or in the lives they have influenced, or in their deeds and works. To say that Shakespeare is immortal in the sense that his plays will always be read is not really to speak about the man

Shakespeare at all but about his ideas. The quality of this life is quite different if it is seen as a school for eternity as well as being good in itself. Surely the idea that man's deeds have eternal significance is not to be treated lightly as a kind of optional belief or pious opinion. Belief in the Hereafter is deeply rooted in Judaism and to reject it is to impoverish and despiritualize Judaism itself.

'The general tendency among modern Jews who do believe in an Afterlife is to place the stress on the immortality of the soul rather than on the resurrection of the dead.'

As can be seen from the above, very brief, outlines of the various religions, a general theme of birth, death and afterlife runs through all of them. Perhaps an appropriate way to end this chapter on religious attitudes towards reincarnation would be to draw attention to the fact that in the Bible it was suggested that John the Baptist had come in the spirit of Elijah, in other words, that John the Baptist was the reincarnation of Elijah.

It would appear that at the time of the ministry of Jesus on earth, the idea of reincarnation must have been an acceptable one, even amongst His disciples, because when Jesus asked them who they thought He was they gave various answers, all indicating that the idea of a soul of a dead person coming back to earth in a different physical body was not foreign or strange to them. From the fact that the disciples answered Him as they did, it is clear that a belief in reincarnation must have been an everyday part of their lives.